GW00497952

MARINERS OF BRITTANY

"Terre-Neuvas" at Saint-Servan

MARINERS *of* BRITTANY

WRITTEN AND ILLUSTRATED
BY PETER F. ANSON

J. M. DENT AND SONS LTD.
LONDON

First published 1931
This edition 1974

© Foreword J. M. Dent & Sons Ltd 1974

Made in Great Britain
by Unwin Brothers Limited
The Gresham Press, Old Woking, Surrey
A member of the Staples Printing Group
for J. M. Dent & Sons Limited
Aldine House · Albemarle Street · London

ISBN 0 460 04192 4

CONTENTS

LIST OF ILLUSTRATIONS

LIST OF ILLUSTRATIONS vii

MAPS

Pointe Saint-Mathieu, Monument to the Seamen of Brittany

AUTHOR'S PREFACE

THIS book makes no pretence of being either a guide-book or a nautical history of Brittany. It is nothing more than a superficial and extremely inadequate description of the Breton race in its maritime aspects: impressions of the sea-girt land, its seafaring people, their lives ashore and afloat, their manners and customs, religion and folk-lore, their fishing vessels and other craft.

I regret that my treatment of this subject is not so exhaustive or so detailed as it deserves to be. Every writer who has ever attempted to obtain accurate and reliable information about Brittany and its maritime life has experienced the same difficulty as I have: the average Breton has both an innate prejudice and fear against revealing himself to a stranger, even if one asks him a simple and straightforward question such as the measurements of his boat! When one is handicapped by an ignorance of his language and obliged to converse in French a further obstacle is imposed to mutual intercourse and understanding. But I am consoled to read that even such a "Breton—bretonnant" as Anatole Le Braz confesses to having been confronted by the same embarrassment when he started to collect the old stories of the country-side from the fisherfolk of Port Blanc.

The coast of Brittany is gradually being transformed into one long succession of bathing resorts and *plages*. No matter where one goes in summer months, except perhaps on the Iles-de-Sein, Ouessant and Groix, can one escape the sound of the ubiquitous motor charabanc with its load of trippers and tourists. Belle-Isle, for instance, has become a second Isle of Wight or Isle of Man, the Ile-de-Bréhat almost a suburb of Paris. One wonders how long it will be before the old Brittany disappears altogether. Everything is changing with an alarming rapidity; manners, customs,

ix

boats, and methods of fishing, even though it would be hard to find a more naturally conservative race than the Breton.

In ten years' time I expect that the types of fishing craft I have shown in these illustrations will be utterly extinct.

I must thank all who have helped me in writing these pages. It is not possible to mention them all by name, but I must single out the following: Monsieur H. de Penfentenyo, administrateur-délégué of the Société des Œuvres de Mer; Monsieur J. de Thézac, founder of the "Abris du Marin"; Monsieur le chanoine Pol Aubert, aumônier de l'Ecole Navale at Brest; Monsieur l'abbé Havard, editor of the paper *La Jeunesse Maritime*; Monsieur Jean Véron, aspirant de marine; the Rev. Père Lebret, O.P., ancien lieutenant de vaisseau; the Rev. Père Colomban Lefebvre, O.M. Cap., ancien capitaine de corvette; Monsieur l'abbé Bossennec, curé of Ouessant; Monsieur le chanoine Saillour, curé doyen of Paimpol; Monsieur l'abbé Jacq, vicaire of the Ile-de-Sein; Monsieur l'abbé Le Scao, Guilvinec; Monsieur Jean Cabon, Concarneau, Methuen & Co. for permission to paraphrase several stories from W. Branch Johnson's *Folk Tales of Brittany*, and others who have advised, helped, encouraged, and criticized both my drawings and the letterpress.

PETER F. ANSON.

DÉDICACE

Aux marins de Bretagne.

C'est à vous, mes chers amis des côtes d'Armor, de Saint-Malo à Saint-Nazaire, que je veux dédier ce livre.

Depuis bien longtemps déjà, j'avais eu l'idée d'écrire sur les marins, fils de votre Bretagne. Elle m'était venue cette idée alors que j'habitais au milieu des rochers de la petite île de Caldey, au sud du pays de Galles. Peut-être avez-vous passé devant cette île et son phare? Plusieurs d'entre vous ont eu l'occasion d'aller prendre du charbon à Cardiff ou à Swansea. Autrefois, il y a bien des siècles de cela, vivaient dans ce pays les moines Celtes qui ont donné leurs noms à tant de vos paroisses : Saint Samson, Saint Pol de Léon, Saint Ildut, Saint Teilo, Saint Magloire, Saint Gildas, et bien d'autres. J'avais alors souvent pensé à ces moines marins, et les voyais montant sur leurs frêles barques, puis descendant sur vos côtes bretonnes où ils convertirent vos ancêtres à la foi chrétienne, qu'avec votre belle ténacité vous avez depuis ce temps gardée sans tache.

Et j'aimais à rêver qu'un jour, moi aussi, je m'embarquerais peut-être pour un pareil voyage . . . non plus pour vous convertir toutefois ; j'aimais à penser que j'irais voir *ce coin de pierre au cœur de l'océan*, et pénétrer quelque peu dans la vie de cette race de hardis marins répandue au long des côtes de la Bretagne.

Pourtant je dois dire que ce fut, non pas sur la côte d'Emeraude, mais sur la côte d'Azur, toute ensoleillée, que je fis d'abord votre connaissance. Ce fut à Toulon, dans la villa Jeanne d'Arc, la maison du Marin et du Soldat, où au milieu de vous j'ai passé tant de jours heureux.

Il y a bien près de dix ans que je vous vis là pour la première fois.

Et le temps, les années ne m'ont pas fait oublier vos noms, vous : Yves Kerbrat, François Gargadennec, ni vous Alain Thomas, Kerdoncuff . . . et bien d'autres, car je ne puis ici vous nommer tous.

Vous veniez de tous les coins de la Bretagne; il y en avait du Finistère, du Morbihan, des Côtes-du-Nord, du pays malouin, mais tous vous étiez remplis du même amour de la mer, de votre race et de votre pays. Et chez vous parfois, quelle nostalgie sous le beau soleil de Provence, pour le ciel gris, la pluie et le brouillard des jours d'hiver de l'Armorique.

Vous vous rappelez les visites que nous faisions ensemble à vos "pays" exilés comme vous; vous vous rappelez les crêpes chaudes que l'on mangeait avec le beurre doré qui venait d'arriver tout frais de Bretagne?

Parfois encore, on se rendait en chœur aux petits cafés du quai Cronstadt. Ils n'étaient pas seulement que de nom, mais bien en réalité, le "*Rendez-vous des Bretons*," le "*Bar de Brest*." Là, dans cette atmosphère toute de famille et d'abandon, vous pouviez oublier que je ne comprenais pas votre langue bretonne et vous vous racontiez, entre vous seuls, vos souvenirs. Mais pendant que vous parliez, ces sons inconnus, qui frappaient mon oreille sans se faire entendre, me transportaient loin du brillant soleil de la Provence, au milieu des vagues de l'océan gris des tempêtes, et j'entendais ses lames furieuses déferler avec un bruit de tonnerre sur les rochers de granit de la côte bretonne.

Mais la conversation ne tardait pas à revenir vers moi sous un visage connu, et j'apprenais là des "Grésillons" les mystères de la pêche au thon; les gas de Douarnenez et de Tréboul me racontaient les exaspérants conflits entre usiniers et sardiniers; je vivais avec les marins de Paimpol et de Saint-Malo la dure et périlleuse vie du pêcheur aux prises avec la terrible mer au large de l'Islande ou sur les Grands Bancs de Terre-Neuve.

Puis, lorsque dans les rues de Toulon passait une blanche coiffe bretonne, comme une pâle fleur du Nord transplantée et devenue éblouissante sous le clair soleil du Midi, vous vous exclamiez: "Regardez, en voilà une de chez nous . . . celle-là, c'est la coiffe de Pont-Aven . . . voici, ma foi, une 'touken' Trégorroise." Et, en murmurant ces paroles, il y avait toujours dans le ton de la voix, cette je ne sais quelle envie de revoir le pays, cette indéfinissable nostalgie qui est au cœur de tout Celte.

Je me suis fait aussi un devoir de me rendre avec l'aumônier de la marine auprès du lit de vos camarades, à l'Hôpital de Saint-Mandrier. Puis, le soir, quel plaisir pour moi d'accompagner les chansons de chez vous, sur le vieux piano éclopé de la "Maison du Marin."

Ce sont là de vieux souvenirs, mais vous vous rappelez, n'est-ce pas?

Il s'est pourtant depuis, passé bien des années. Depuis, j'ai visité, j'ai fouillé toute la côte bretonne de Nantes à Cancale. Et je crois qu'il y a bien peu de ports, petits ou grands, où je n'ai pris des esquisses et dessiné quelques vues de vos barques.

Mais pourrez-vous comprendre mon livre? Un livre anglais, écrit en "Saoz."

Oui, bien certainement! Les choses de la mer vous sont si familières! Comment ne les comprendriez-vous pas? Qu'est-ce que pourriez bien en ignorer? De la mer et des choses de la mer, vous avez l'amour dans le sang. Vous comprendrez donc ces pages, même écrites en Anglais, car vous y trouverez toujours quelque dessin qui vous parlera une langue que vous savez, et que savent tous les marins. J'aime à penser que vous les regarderez avec plaisir, ces impressions des choses de chez vous.

Et si cela se réalise, je ne croirai pas avoir perdu mon temps.

PETER F. ANSON.

Pardon des Islandais, le 8 décembre 1930.

FOREWORD

THE Breton peninsula is a land of relatively subdued relief, low hills and ridges, plateaus and gently shelving coastal plains, only occasionally deeply dissected by streams and rivers. Around the coasts of Brittany the seas are renowned for their strong currents and great tidal range with large areas of shore laid bare at low tide as in the Golfe du Morbihan and the Baie du Mont St Michel. The long tidal estuaries allow small ships deep into the land and have always served as a nursery for mariners. Today, Quimper, Pont Aven, Morlaix, Vannes and many other small ports some kilometres from the open sea are frequented mostly, but not entirely, by yachts, motor cruisers and other pleasure boats, although a few fishing vessels are still to be found and there is a little coastal trade. The fishing industry has become chiefly concentrated at a number of larger ports such as Douarnenez and Concarneau.

It was to this remote and impoverished region with its poor soils but mild climate, that peoples from south-western Britain emigrated, probably from the late fourth-century A.D. onwards, turning the former Gallo-Roman province of Armorica into a westward looking nation with its contacts, culture, population and church closely linked with those of the British Isles. These people were Celts, speaking a language from which modern Welsh, Cornish and Breton have evolved. Western Brittany, in spite of recent vicissitudes, remains a Celtic speaking region and although today French is spoken in addition, Breton remains the working language of the farm and fishing boat as well as being the language of the home. Many a Breton finds it difficult to describe his life and work adequately in French.

The invasion from the north was not the first, for an earlier civilisation had entered from the south with the expansion of prehistoric trade along the western seaways. This was the so-called megalithic culture of the Neolithic period which left behind thousands of great stone monuments of which the most impressive are probably the *alignements* of Carnac, but *menhirs* and *dolmens* are found over the whole peninsula, the greatest number being grouped around the Golfe du Morbihan, testifying to the continuity of human occupance. With the coming of the Bretons in the early Dark Ages, there came also the Celtic saints from Cornwall and Wales. Churches, which often became the centres of future settlements, were founded and dedicated to St Pol, St Sampson, St Cadoc, St Maudez, St Iltud and many others.

A distinction is usually drawn between the interior, Arcoët (the land of the wood) still heavily wooded in places, and the coastal lowlands, Armor (the land by the sea), where more fertile soils and the proximity to the ocean have led to generally greater prosperity. The predominantly agricultural population dwelt, and continues to dwell, entirely in hamlets and isolated farms. In spite of wide variation, the dense pattern of settlement has been a well-known characteristic of Brittany until recent times, but since the end of the Second World War, and particularly during the last fifteen years, the effects of economic change and the common market agricultural policy have led to changes which in some places can only be described as cataclysmic. The attraction of the larger towns and more remunerative industrial work has resulted in rapid rural depopulation and the abandonment of small farms and cottages by the younger people, leaving behind an ageing population. As the older generation passes, whole hamlets have become deserted, particularly in the more difficult areas such as the Monts d'Arrée. Where once a hamlet consisted of ten or a dozen small farms all actively worked, now only one or two may remain. In the coastal area, the pattern is sometimes little different, especially in the remoter regions of the west. On the islands, notably Ile d'Ouessant, and the Crozon and Penmarc'h peninsulas where a dense population once subsisted on open-field agriculture, fishing and sea-faring, large areas of land now lie abandoned with scrub spreading to obscure the old field boundaries. The tiny houses and cottages have either been handed down to a younger generation to use as holiday homes or they have been purchased by outsiders so that whole hamlets come to life for only a

few weeks in the summer.   Until recent times the way of life over
much of Brittany had advanced little beyond that of the Middle
Ages and in parts of the peninsula life can fairly be said to have
remained in a proto-historic phase.   The plough was still unknown
on Ile d'Ouessant at the time the land fell out of cultivation after the
second world war.   Tillage was by the spade, as it was also in other
parts of the west and the chief source of fuel on certain islands, in the
absence of timber, was turf and cow-dung.

   The coastal zone has always been less remote than the interior, and
more heavily populated ever since the land was first settled.   The
peninsula has played an important role in the western seaways since
Neolithic peoples spread northwards from Iberia.   Contacts between Brittany, Cornwall, Wales and Ireland have always been close
and in earlier ages when travel by land was hazardous, maritime
activity was intense.   These early sailors journeyed in boats of
wicker frame covered in skins, probably similar to the Irish
curragh of today, as well as in coracles, dug-out boats and small
wooden ships.   This outward looking tradition of maritime activity
continues and Breton sailors and fishermen travel widely.   Whilst
in some areas the tradition is for the menfolk to serve in the *Marine
Nationale*, in others service is usually in the *marine marchande*.   This
experience of the outside world gives the coastal areas a degree of
worldliness totally absent from the interior.   During the present
century many of the coastal towns and fishing ports have become
important holiday resorts and the tourist trade has led to expansion
and increased prosperity.   New villas of whitewashed *beton* with
slate roofs and granite dressings are springing up everywhere and
in the absence of adequate planning control threaten the natural
beauty of the coastal zone.   Brittany is changing dramatically and
rapidly, but many of the old customs and practices may still be seen
by the observant, and the heritage of material culture is ever present.

   Peter Anson writes of Brittany between the wars when the lives of
both cultivators and fishers were still governed by traditions thousands of years old.   He brings out vividly the variety in the construction of boats and the variations in the patterns of fishing.
Working in the 1920s he was able to record not only customs and

superstitions still practised and believed, but also those recently abandoned or in decline although preserved in the memory. It is a tragedy that so little work has been done on the folk-life of a province which ranks with the other Celtic countries as one of the great repositories of ancient customs and practices, for it is now almost too late. This book must remain a valuable contribution to the study of the folk-life of western Europe and we should be grateful to Peter Anson for recording much that would otherwise have been lost.

GWYN I MEIRION-JONES.
Principal lecturer in Geography

Sir John Cass School of Science and Technology
City of London Polytechnic, 1973.

CHAPTER I

INTRODUCTION—"ARMOR," COUNTRY OF THE SEA

BRITTANY, before everything else, is a maritime country, a land of seafarers. Its children are familiar from infancy with the sight and sound of the waves. They are charmed and fascinated by the ocean. The figure of a woman and her lover is worn threadbare, but it is true that the sea lures the Breton to her. She woos him, and he responds to her charms. He asks nothing better than to be allowed to live with her for her, and by her. It is not a matter of material gain or sordid interest. His work will be hard, his reward insignificant in comparison. He is drawn to the sea by its vastness, by the sense of the unknown, by its danger: everything in fact that appeals to all that is best and human in man. The sea means everything for the Breton who is born and bred on the coast (and indeed for thousands more whose homes are inland). The children are never so happy as when they are playing on the seashore, better still when they can clamber on board some vessel and feel the deck beneath their feet. The grown-up man, when not at sea, spends most of his time on shore gazing out over the ocean, dreaming of his next voyage, and impatient for the moment when he will again feel the movement of deep water beneath him. The sea is all in all to him; she is a capricious and fickle mistress. The Breton is her lover, sometimes her master, but more often her victim. She bewitches him with promises. She occasionally shares with him her riches, but in return she demands his body, his soul, and his life.

The original name of Brittany, *Armor, Armorica,* means the "country of the sea." The ocean has left its mark on the land wherever one goes. Even several miles inland, where the sea can be neither seen nor heard, one realizes that it is not very far off.

The air has a salt tang in it. The stunted vegetation is always bent with a wind that blows the greater part of the year from the direction of the sea.

Creeks and tidal rivers eat their way into the heart of the country-side. There is not one of them that does not boast a little *port* where one finds moored fishing craft, cargo boats, "dundees," "goëlettes," and large, broad-beamed vessels laden with sand or kelp. Vannes, Quimper, Landerneau, Morlaix, Lannion, Tré-guier, Saint-Brieuc, Dinan—to mention but a few of the more important—are characteristic examples of Breton ports that are to be found away from the sea on the estuaries of rivers.

This is but one aspect of the maritime life of Brittany. Making one's way to the coast of Finistère, where the granite cliffs are exposed year in, year out, to the fierce assault of the ocean, great waves that roll in unchecked for thousands of miles from another continent, one is confronted by another picture. There can be few places in the world where one is so conscious of the terror of the sea, as when gazing out from the Pointe du Raz over the reef of rocks that are all that is left of the submerged land where once stood the mysterious Ville d'Ys famous in the legendary lore of Armor. Visit any of the outlying islands—Ouessant, Sein, Groix, Belle-Ile, the Glénans—and you will realize still better what the sea means to Brittany, and why its history has been so inseparably bound up with the ocean.

As you sail across the Passage du Fromveur or the Raz de Sein when the currents are so fierce and so rapid that they look more like whirlpools, you will find yourself instinctively repeating the prayer that comes so readily to the lips of every Breton seafarer:

"Protégez-moi, Seigneur, ma barque est si petite et la mer est si grande."

The mariners of Brittany can be numbered in thousands. They belong to all classes of society. They are of all ages and both sexes, for all along the coast from Mont Saint-Michel to Saint-Nazaire the women who earn their living by the sea are almost as numerous as the men.

In the olden days when sail was the only means of navigation, the greater number of Breton seamen were employed either in fishing or in cargo boats: "voiliers," "goëlettes," "chasse-marées," "bricks," "dundees," making comparatively short voyages around the coast from port to port. To-day this coasting trade has greatly diminished. The majority of men are engaged either in the sardine or Newfoundland fisheries, or else serving in the *marine de guerre*, on ocean liners, or on long-distance cargo-steamers.

About fifty thousand men are said to be engaged in the Breton fishing industry. On the north coast every village has a group of fishermen, the boats and gear used being for the most part of a very old-fashioned sort. You come across a little group of houses, generally built of grey granite, often whitewashed, sometimes nestling beneath overhanging trees on the shores

BOATS ON THE ILE-D'OUESSANT

of some tidal creek, or exposed to all the four winds of heaven on the edge of the sea. Little houses huddling against each other, as if for mutual protection, always with their windows facing inland and not seawards: a significant proof of the force of the storms of winter. Around the doors are heaps of shells and fish-bones. Nets are hung over walls and fences to dry in the sun. At low tide men, women, and children go down among the rocks to gather bait. The actual fishing seldom occupies more than three or four hours.

The boats used are of a primitive character, without decks and carrying a lug-sail and oars. They seldom go far off, hardly ever out of sight of land. The Breton seaman is naturally conservative, and those engaged in the *petite pêche* are the most conservative of all: what was good enough for their fathers and grandfathers is good enough for them. But life under such conditions is precarious; sometimes fish is abundant, other times scarce, and it is not easy to feed and clothe a large family if such is your sole means of livelihood. In these days, when the cost of living has increased so much in comparison with what it was fifty years ago, the prospects of a Breton fisherman of this class are not encouraging.

The chief centres of the *grande pêche* are Saint-Malo, Cancale, Binic, Paimpol, Camaret, and Lorient-Kéroman, above all the last-named, where a magnificent port on the most modern lines has been opened in recent years.

Saint-Malo is the centre of the Newfoundland cod fisheries. A few boats for the Iceland fisheries are still sent out every year from Paimpol. Camaret is famous for its lobster boats—very familiar sights off the coast of Cornwall. The "Grésillons" (as the men of Groix are called) were the pioneers to fish for tunny in the Bay of Biscay. Their example has been followed by Concarneau, Douarnenez, and other ports, from June to December; for the rest of the year they engage in trawling. But with the creation of the new port of Lorient-Kéroman, "white fishing" on the south coast of Brittany is undergoing a rapid transformation.

The sardine fisheries constitute the chief source of wealth on the south-west coast. The chief ports engaged are Douarnenez, Audierne, Guilvinec, and Concarneau.

Brittany has always been looked upon as the chief recruiting-ground for the French navy. Indeed, one could say with truth that without the mariners of Brittany the *marine de guerre* could not exist. Wherever one goes in Armor one is sure to be confronted by the uniform of a *col bleu* or *quartier-maître* at home on leave. Once I was travelling about the country for nearly three months, seldom passing more than two days without going by train. Never once in that whole period did I find myself on a station platform or

THE CEMETERY, PLOUBAZLANEC
(Graves of sailors who have been lost at sea)

in a railway carriage without meeting the blue uniform and red pompom cap of the *col bleu*. It made me realize more than any printed figures or statistics how vast a number of Bretons there must be in the French navy. One simply could not get away from them. And in every town and village, even those at some distance from the coast, I met old men who bore the unmistakable sign of having been seamen at some time or other. Their button-holes or coats were decorated with a ribbon or medals which told the tale of campaigns in which they had been engaged, of naval engagements near home or abroad, proofs of the part that maritime Brittany has played in the seafaring history of France.

No cemetery along the coast is without its countless graves of those who have followed the sea, and who are now sleeping their last sleep hard by the church where they were baptized and where they were taught the great truths of that Catholic religion, to which most of them have been so loyal and so faithful, even if in their human weakness they have often failed to live up to its moral precepts. In some places, too, you will find cemeteries for those whose bodies do not rest in the graves that are so tenderly cared for: men who have been lost at sea in shipwreck and in storm. These *cimetières des naufragés* are perhaps the most significant proof of the part that the sea plays in the lives of the Bretons, of the victims it demands of them.

The mariners of Brittany have also left a permanent record of their voyages in various parts of North America, particularly in the maritime provinces of Canada, which were largely settled by families from Brittany. Cape Breton Island, off Nova Scotia, is said to have been so called in honour of its Breton discoverers, although some authorities would maintain that the name is derived from Capbreton, a small village on the shores of the Bay of Biscay, north of Bayonne, inhabited by the Basque fishermen who in the sixteenth and seventeenth centuries were among the pioneers of the cod fisheries off the Newfoundland Banks. However, all that we know for certain is that the name, probably the oldest French name in the North American continent, was given to the cape early in the sixteenth century. And what a Breton atmosphere is conjured up by the names of so many towns in French Canada! All along the shores of the Gulf of St. Lawrence one finds oneself in a world that preserves the habits and customs of seventeenth- and eighteenth-century Brittany. If you should find yourself on the little island of Saint-Pierre, near Sydney, Cape Breton, on the feast of Saint Anne, you might well believe you had been transported to the other side of the Atlantic.

On the other hand, when you visit Belle-Ile, off the south coast of Brittany, you will meet descendants of many of the French families who were expelled from Acadie in 1755 by the British conquerors of Canada, the story which has been made celebrated by Longfellow in his poem *Evangeline*.

The famous shrine of Sainte-Anne-de-Beaupré, near Quebec, is said to have been founded by mariners of Brittany in 1620 and is the most frequented place of pilgrimage in North America, the number of persons coming here every year rivalling if not surpassing those who journey to the shrine of Sainte-Anne d'Auray in Brittany.

In later years what a large proportion of the crews of American privateers was made up of Bretons who were only too glad to have the chance of fighting against their hereditary enemies the English!

CHAPTER II

RELIGION AND SOCIAL CONDITIONS AMONG THE MARINERS OF BRITTANY

ONE approaches the subject of the religious and social conditions of the seafarers of Brittany with more than a certain nervousness. It is only too easy for a comparative outsider to form an inaccurate or exaggerated impression of external manifestations of which he may not be in a position to judge the true significance in relation to life as a whole.

Personally I should much prefer to say nothing about the religion of the Breton sailor, for after all it is his own affair, not mine. But on the other hand, since the practice of the Catholic faith plays such an important part in the life of every Breton village, it simply cannot be ignored in any book that professes to deal with the seafaring inhabitant of this country.

About a year ago a questionnaire was widely circulated among the mercantile marine, *marine de guerre*, and fishing communities, in order to try to arrive at some idea regarding the religious situation of the modern French seafarer.[1] The answers received were of great interest. As most of them came from Breton sailors, it will not be out of place to give a brief summary of the opinions arrived at by the comparison of these letters.

Now theoretically about ninety per cent of the mariners of Brittany are Catholics. Most of them have been baptized, most of them have made their first Communion. But how many of them actually keep up the practice of their religion after they go to sea? In the everyday phraseology, how many are *pratiquants*, i.e. hear Mass on Sundays and make their Easter Communion? For this is the minimum obligation to which every Catholic is bound. In the parishes situated on the coast of Brittany it would appear that about two-thirds of the seafaring population

[1] *La Jeunesse Maritime*, July, 1930.

are *pratiquants*, a very high proportion compared with the rest of France. But these are men who are actually living at home and who are largely influenced by public opinion. To stop away from Mass on Sunday, not to go to Communion at Easter, are actions which would put an ordinary Breton fisherman, in a village which has not yet been won over to extreme socialism or communism, outside the pale of respectable society. And his wife takes good care that he observes these conventions so long as he is under her eye.

But what happens when he goes to sea? What happens to the average young Breton when he is serving in the *marine de guerre*? Here again his religious practice is largely influenced by public opinion. The majority of his shipmates make no pretence of obeying even the minimum regulations of the Church to which they profess to belong. True, it requires a certain amount of individual effort, for in the French navy to-day there is no official recognition of any kind of religion—Catholic, Protestant, Jew, or Moslem. So the average Breton, afraid of making himself conspicuous, just ceases to practise his faith. As a certain Breton sailor once expressed it to me: "Quand on est dans la marine, on est en congé avec le bon Dieu—When one is at sea, one takes a holiday from religion." The result of this mentality is that probably not more than five to ten per cent of the Breton seamen continue to practise their religious duties when they go to sea.

Deep down in his heart, the Breton sailor has always been, like every Celt, profoundly religious. His bunk on board ship will be decorated with a little image or picture of Our Lady. He will carry a rosary in his pocket, or wear it around his neck, even if he seldom uses it as an aid to prayer.

The *idea* of Mary, Mother of God, Star of the Sea—a spiritual lighthouse, a heavenly pilot, a divine patroness, a merciful and kind mother who forgives and understands the weakness of human nature—these facts, learnt long ago when he was a tiny boy at his mother's knee, are always somewhere not very far down in his subconsciousness, vaguely yet securely present, and resorted to in moments of danger and distress.

Every one who has visited Brittany will remember the statue of

the Blessed Virgin that stands in a niche over the great gateway
by which one enters the city on landing at Saint-Malo from the
steamer—"Notre-Dame de la Grande Porte," as she is called.
For centuries she has stood there, watching over the "nest of corsairs," as Saint-Malo used to be called. Placed there, high up
above the street, inaccessible, yet visible to all that pass by who
choose to look up, Notre-Dame de la Grande Porte always seems
to me to typify the place that Our Lady has held in the religious
life of the mariners of Brittany for over a thousand years.

In many villages of Brittany it was, and still is, the custom before
the departure of the fishermen and boys for the Newfoundland
Banks to organize a retreat or a mission for them. At the conclusion, a ceremony of consecration or a procession to some favourite
shrine was always part of the programme. Few *Terre - Neuvas*
would venture to embark without a previous visit to Notre-Dame de
Saint-Jouan, Notre-Dame de l'Épine, Notre-Dame de Délivrance,
Notre-Dame du Verger, or some other popular sanctuary in the
neighbourhood. In most villages a special Mass for sailors was
always celebrated before the *départ des Terre-Neuvas* at the altar of
Our Lady in the parish church. During the long summer months,
while the fleets were absent thousands of miles across the Atlantic,
they were not forgotten. Pilgrimages of sweethearts and wives,
mothers and grandmothers, to some favourite shrine went on
continuously, more often in small groups. Go to Notre-Dame du
Verger any day between March and September and you will
seldom find this little sanctuary on the edge of the waves without
its worshippers invoking Our Lady, Star of the Sea, to give a safe
return home to the crews of the "goëlettes," off Newfoundland.

The flames of innumerable votive candles flicker like spiritual
lighthouses before the image of the Mother of God in every village
church along the coast, but more especially in the pilgrimage
shrines of Notre-Dame de l'Epine (Saint-Brieuc), Notre-Dame de la
Landrais (Miniac), Notre-Dame de l'Espérance (Mont Dol), Notre-
Dame des Flots (Rothéneuf), Notre-Dame du Bois-Renou (La
Gouesnière), Notre-Dame de la Garde (Saint-Benoît des Ondes)—
to mention a few in the neighbourhood of Saint-Malo alone.

In the autumn when the fishing is over and the men have returned home, similar pilgrimages of thanksgiving take place. In former times it was no uncommon sight to witness whole crews walking bare-footed along the roads, wearing either their fishermen's oil-skins or dressed in nothing more than shirt and trousers, an act of penitence and gratitude for having been preserved from dangers at sea, and having been brought back safely. A lonely sanctuary exposed to all the gales from the Atlantic is that of Notre-Dame de Bon Voyage at Plogoff, not far from the Pointe du Raz in Finistère. On the day of the "Pardon" (second Sunday in July), it'was formerly the custom for the fishermen of Audierne and the adjacent villages to walk barefoot all the way there, and if they had been preserved from any great danger or shipwreck, wearing the same clothes as when their escape took place. Sometimes they would even jump into the sea and walk to the church dripping wet! The story is told of certain sailors about a hundred years ago, who made a vow during a great storm at sea that, if they were saved, they would climb the spire of Notre-Dame du Folgoat and let themselves hang head downwards with their arms extended.[1]

The fisherfolk of the Ile-de-Sein, which on account of its isolation has so far escaped the influence of modern indifference to religion and secular teaching, are still famous for the long pilgrimages they make to shrines of Our Lady. It is a never-to-be-forgotten sight to watch them embark for the Pardon of Notre-Dame de Plogoff, with their boats all decorated with flags and banners. There are few sailors on the Ile-de-Sein who have not managed to make at least one pilgrimage to Lourdes, with their wives and families.

At the mouth of the River Odet, opposite Benodet, stands a little chapel dedicated to the Blessed Virgin, adjacent to the village of Sainte-Marine. In bygone days the custom was that, when a crew found themselves windbound in any of the neighbouring ports, two of the men were sent on foot to Sainte-Marine to ask the intercession of Our Lady so that the wind might change. They first of all swept out and thoroughly cleaned the chapel, and then collected the dust and threw it in the direction they wanted the

---

[1] Mabasque, *Notions sur les Côtes-du-Nord*, vol. i, p. 308.

wind to blow. The relations of those who were waiting for the return of their menfolk used to observe the same practice in this chapel.[1]

After the Blessed Virgin there is no more popular saint among the mariners of Brittany than Saint Anne. The origin of the Breton devotion to Saint Anne is difficult to explain. Many authorities maintain that Saint Anne, mother of Our Lady, is merely a substitute for Ahés, the pagan goddess of the sea, whom the people of Armor used to worship before their conversion to Christianity. Here, in brief, is the ordinary version of the legend of Saint Anne, as related in Brittany.

Saint Anne was born in Brittany of a noble family. Her husband treated her with great cruelty, and finding herself with child, she fled to the sea, where an angel guided her to a ship. After a long voyage she landed at Jaffa, whence she made her way to Nazareth. Soon afterwards she gave birth to a baby girl to whom she gave the name of Mary. When the latter was fifteen years of age she was espoused to a carpenter named Joseph, and Saint Anne prayed to be allowed to return to her native Brittany. Once more she was miraculously transported across the sea under the protection of an angel. On her arrival she found her husband was dead. She gave away all her property and ended her days in a little hermitage overlooking the Bay of Douarnenez on the spot where now stands the chapel of Sainte-Anne de la Palud.

This famous sanctuary, whose Pardon takes place every year on the last Sunday in August, is the original centre of devotion to Saint Anne in Brittany. However, since 1623, the popular *cultus* of the saint has been largely diverted to Sainte-Anne d'Auray, a little village not far from Auray, in Morbihan, where a half-witted peasant, Yves Nicolazic, had a vision in which he was told to have built a chapel on the spot where a shrine of Saint Anne was supposed to have existed since the tenth century. His neighbours declared he was mad, but when to their astonishment he dug up an old and mutilated image of the saint, they began to think there might be something to be said for his visions. Pilgrims soon began to

[1] L. F. Sauvé, in *Mélusine*, vol. ii, col. 207.

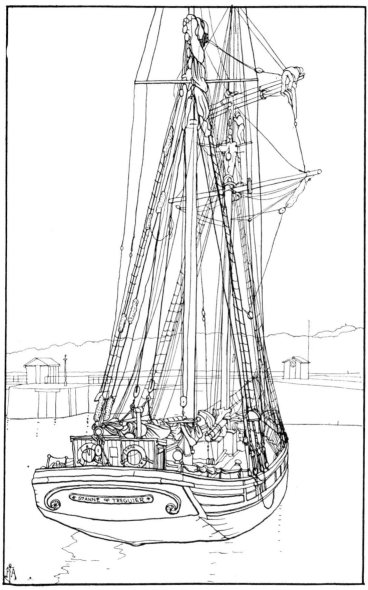

"Goëlette," Sainte-Anne, Paimpol

flock to the spot: a chapel was built, and ever since Sainte-Anne d'Auray has been the most frequented shrine in the whole of Brittany. The Pardon on 25th July attracts vast crowds. One might well describe Sainte-Anne d'Auray as the spiritual capital of Armor.

Devotion to Sainte Anne among Breton sailors is generally expressed in the form of a "vow" made to her during a storm at sea or other occasions of danger when they promise to make a pilgrimage to one of her shrines if they are saved. Examples of these *vœux* have been recorded for the past four or five hundred years. At least a hundred and twelve miraculous favours granted to sailors are to be found in the archives of Sainte-Anne d'Auray between the years 1627 and 1657 alone. The notable feature of these miracles, as related by the sailors, is their instantaneous character. "The tempest ceased as soon as we made our vow." "Without any hope of being saved, we prayed to the glorious Saint Anne, and immediately the sea was calm." "The moment after we had made our vow, to the great astonishment of the crew, the storm decreased." "A fog sprang up at midday, I prayed to God and Sainte Anne; very soon after the mist cleared away and we saw rocks ahead of us and were saved, much to the astonishment of the Huguenots, who could not help saying that there was no human explanation of the matter." Such are a few typical examples taken from the archives of Sainte-Anne d'Auray.

More often than not the *vœu* takes the form of a definite promise to make a pilgrimage barefoot and bareheaded, dressed only in shirt and trousers, and fasting on bread and water. Even non-Catholics were sometimes moved to invoke Sainte Anne in moments of danger. The archives of the sanctuary of Auray (vol. i, p. 316) have a quaint story of a Scottish Presbyterian advocate who made a pilgrimage to Sainte Anne, bringing the price of a barrel of wine as a votive offering, because he had been preserved from drowning at sea! The *trésor* at Sainte-Anne d'Auray contains innumerable votive offerings presented by sailors: pictures and models of ships, flags, bits of clothing, medals and decorations, silver lamps, and so on. From the year 1628, when Jean le Net relates how his ship was driven by a wind of terrific force from the coast of Newfoundland to the river of Vannes in less than thirteen days (when usually it took a month) and no harm befell either the ship or the crew, until the year 1900, when the Breton sailors in China were preserved from the attacks of the Boxers, there is one long succession of stories of the miraculous intervention of Sainte Anne on behalf of seafarers. Can one be surprised that *le marin Breton* still retains such an intense faith in her motherly care for him in face of such evidence of past favours?

There are so many local fêtes or "Pardons" connected more or less intimately with the life of the mariners of Brittany that it would be impossible to deal with them all in the limits of this book.

The Breton Pardon is a festival held in some church or chapel, accompanied by picturesque ceremonies both of a religious and secular character. Pilgrims arrive in crowds from all parts of the neighbourhood for the purposes of devotion. Related to the "Pardons" and similar in character are the "Blessings of the sea," which take place in almost every village on the coast of Brittany. Here is a brief list, far from complete, of those Pardons which are associated more especially with the sea and seafaring life:

Combrit (second Sunday in September); *Concarneau* (Sunday after 14th September); *Groix* (Blessing of the Sea, 24th July); *Paimpol* (Pardon of the "Islandais" in February); *Roscoff* (Sainte Barbe, third Monday of July, 15th August); *Le Conquet* (Blessing of the Sea, July); *Cancale* (Notre-Dame du Verger, 15th August)

The number of local saints to whom devotion is paid by the mariners of Brittany is so vast that it would take too long to mention all of them, much more to give anything like an adequate account of their lives and legends and all the extraordinary tales of their miraculous intervention on behalf of their seafaring compatriots in times of danger. We cannot do more than give a few of the more important.

Saint Clement, Saint Brieuc, Saint Lunaire, Saint Jacut, and Saint Cast are very popular on the coast between Dinard and Cap Fréhel. Saint Brieuc has his clients, while around Paimpol and Tréguier the honours are shared by Saint Yves, Saint Gildas, Saint

Gonéry, and Saint Liboubane. Perros-Guirec and Ploumanac'h venerate Saint Guirec. Around Roscoff Saint Paul Aurelian (Pol de Léon) comes easily first, but Sainte Barbe also has a certain *cultus*. Saint John the Baptist is popular on the coast north-east of Morlaix, owing to the fact that his finger is preserved at Saint-Jean du Doigt. On the north coast of Finistère no particular saints would seem to be venerated by sailors and fishermen—except perhaps Saint Iltyd and Saint Paul Aurelian. On the Isle of Ouessant, Saint Paul Aurelian is likewise very popular.

Saint Evette has looked after the fishermen of Audierne ever since she was miraculously saved from shipwreck near Plozévet. Farther south around Penmarch, Saint Guénolé shares the devotion of seafarers with Saint Viaud, Saint Tronoân, and Saint Tromeur. On the south coast of Brittany, until we get to the Golfe du Morbihan, no saints seem to stand out conspicuously. But among the fishermen of that district Saint Gildas is certainly the favourite saint.

One of the most interesting of all the Pardons directly connected with the sea in Brittany is that which still takes place on 24th June, Saint John the Baptist's Day, off the Ile-de-Groix. Here is a picturesque description of this function as it was celebrated nearly a hundred years ago: "The fishing-boats of all the adjacent parishes went in procession to take part in this solemn ceremony, and to invoke Notre-Dame de l'Armor that the sardines might be abundant and of good quality. Crowded with men, women, and children dressed in their Sunday clothes was a vast fleet of every sort of craft. At the head of each "squadron" sailed the boat in which were the clergy, their vestments making a brilliant note of colour in the sunshine, the cross held up aloft and the banner of each parish waving in the breeze. Having arrived near the middle of the strait which separates the Ile-de-Groix from the mainland, the sea was blessed in turn by all the priests who were on board the boats, accompanied by the singing of chants and hymns by the onlookers, together with fervent ejaculations to 'Notre Dame' and 'Madame Sainte Anne.'"[1]

At Paimpol in former times the blessing of the fishing-fleet before

[1] L. Kérardven, *Guionvac'h* (1835), pp. 80-5.

ILE-DE-BÂTZ
(Church of Saint-Paul Aurelian)

its departure for Iceland, the Pardon des Islandais, must have been a marvellous sight.   To-day it has lost its original character owing to the gradual disappearance of the famous old schooners.

But even more imposing was the Pardon des Terre-Neuvas at Saint-Malo, which is still one of the most impressive religious functions connected with the sea and ships to be found anywhere in the world.   The sight of the great basin at Saint-Malo, filled with three-masted barquentines decorated with flags and bunting, the long quays crowded with spectators, the crew of each vessel hanging up aloft on to points of vantage so as to get a better view, the excitement and emotion when the Cardinal Archbishop of Rennes, surrounded by his clergy in their vestments, embarks on a launch and slowly cruises round the basin, blessing every vessel in turn, is something which once seen can never be forgotten.   It would seem likely that in a few years more it may be a relic of the past, for steam and motor will have finally triumphed over sail. At Douarnenez and Audierne, before the fishermen had abandoned their childlike confidence in the supernatural and the teaching of their priests, and had been converted to communism and an extreme form of socialism of an almost revolutionary character, it was a common sight during the summer months for rows of boats to be moored alongside the quays, waiting to be blessed, not only once but many times during the same season, in order that their labour might be profitable.

We shall refer later to the superstitious fears of the Audierne sailors towards *le Bosj*, the evil spirit which does such harm to the fishing, especially to the lobster-pots.   In order to break the spell which he puts upon a boat, the only remedy was to have her blessed by the priest.   So she would be cleaned up and decorated with flags and banners and anchored in the harbour.   Followed by a crowd of fishermen, their wives and families, the priest would embark from the quay and be rowed out to the vessel.   The religious ceremony completed, the "patron" would produce a bottle of brandy and pour out a glassful for the priest who was obliged to drink it.   The bottle was then passed round to each of the crew in turn, and was handed across to the adjacent boats, should there be anything left. The priest was rowed ashore, the anchor raised, and the vessel put out to sea. As a recompense for his services the priest was always given the finest lobster caught.[1]

At Audierne it was believed that Sainte Evette often appeared on the sea on the day of her pardon. Old sailors were convinced they had seen her resplendent in silk and gold, sitting on the trough in which she had long ago been preserved from shipwreck, floating across the bay during the procession. No "Audiernois" was ever known to have been lost at sea if he had remembered to invoke Sainte Evette in the moment of danger.[2]

At one time nearly all the vessels sailing from Breton ports boasted a name in some way connected with religion: "terre-neuvas," "sardiniers," "thonniers," "dundees," — there was no exception to this rule. One would come across: *L'Immaculée Conception*, *Saint-Antoine de Padoue*, *Stella Matutina*, *Saint-Yves*, *Notre-Dame de Lourdes* (and a great many other *Notre-Dames*), *Petit Jésus*, *Sainte-Anne*, *Angelus*, *Gloire à Dieu*, *Sauveur du Monde*, etc.

But in these days, especially in the ports of Douarnenez and Audierne, religious names are no longer popular, for communism and socialism are rampant among the fishermen. And this does not mean an adherence to a certain political party, but a definite antagonism towards everything suggestive of Catholicism or Christianity in any form. So you will now come across boats named *Lénin*, *Jean Jaurès*, *Libre Penseur*, *Lutte pour Vie*, *Socialiste*; or of a more neutral character: *Minerve*, *Mont-Kemmel*, *Vagabonde*, *Ondine*, *Albatros*, while around the quays of the Breton seaports the walls are plastered with notices of meetings and *réunions* of the Communist, Socialist, and Republican parties, and *syndicats de gens de mer*—all of which are significant of the change which has taken place in the character and outlook of the mariners of Brittany within the past fifty years.

There is a continual strife between capital and labour; between the fishermen and the factory owners. When the fiery Celtic temperament escapes from the only external authority which has hitherto managed to control it, the Catholic Church (and that not

[1] H. le Carguet, in *Revue des Traditions Populaires*, vol. iv, p. 537.
[2] H. le Carguet, *Société archéologique du Finistère*, 1899, pp. 195, 199.

without difficulty!), there is no knowing to what lengths it may not go, nor what excesses it may not indulge in.

And to what alarming excesses it does go, if only in the matter of drink! There are few Breton sailors who seem able to resist the temptation to consume more alcoholic liquor, so that they become little less than savages when under its influence.

Few people attempt to deny this accusation. Some of them try to excuse the sailor for his weakness on account of the hardness of his life: that alcohol is necessary for him. Priests have said to me: "Well, after all, it's no good denying the fishermen *do* drink more than they ought to. *Mais ils sont de braves gens, et l'ivrognerie n'est pas un péché mortel.*" One refers to it, because it affects both the physique and the moral of this wonderful race of seafarers. What is going to be the effect on future generations? To make matters worse, since the war the price of cider has gone up so enormously that it has become too expensive a drink for the average fisherman. He has to content himself with a cheap red wine of the worst quality, often heavily doctored, to which he adds a smaller quantity of brandy — either mixed together or drunk separately. And the number of gallons of these liquids consumed by the crew of the average sardine boat is quite incredible. Drink has become the curse of the Breton sailor. Various efforts have been made to combat it, but so far most of them have been ineffectual. The "Abris du Marin," established in eleven fishing centres by Monsieur J. de Thézac, have done more good than anything else, but there are hundreds of men who never enter their doors.

To quote a writer who knows the Breton seaman far more intimately than I do, thanks to the long years he has spent yachting and fishing in their company[1]:

"The *buvette* has become a habit. In Concarneau it is the custom, the fashion, to be drunk; the fisherman who is not drunk is looked upon as an eccentric—a poor fellow, anyway. But so hard is his life at sea that one cannot be other than tolerant with the excesses of these Concarneau fishermen ashore; though the annual

[1] Leslie Richardson, *Brittany and the Loire*, p. 125.

Concarneau from Passage-Lanriec

consumption of alcohol at Concarneau—ten quarts a head—is, to say the least of it, excessive.

"On the Sunday nights, when the fishing is good, the men are hunted out of the *buvettes*, and sent on board, to be ready for the Monday morning's fishing. Not a few fall splash into the harbour on their way aboard, and exciting scenes are sometimes to be witnessed."

And what Captain Richardson describes at Concarneau applies equally well to nearly every other port around the coast of Brittany, as I know only too well by my own experience.

But drunkenness is no new vice in Brittany. As far back as the sixteenth century we find references to it. During the eighteenth century the civil and religious authorities were often making attempts to combat the effects of drink. "Plus occidit gula quam gladio," wrote the rector of Guenrouët in regard to his parishioners. Yet at the same time we find other writers pleading the hardness of a sailor's life demands a little indulgence in alcoholic liquor: "Les fatigues de nos travaux très durs, rendent un verre de vin ou d'eau-de-vie nécessaires."

From the ports of Brest and Lorient petitions were sent to Louis XIV that he would reduce the tax on brandy to thirty sous a bottle. Despite the heavy taxes the consumption of drink increased, largely owing to the growth of smuggling.

During the eighteenth century we find frequent references to the enormous number of *cabarets* and *débits* in the ports of Brittany. Many of them were kept by Irishmen! At Morlaix there was a famous bar on the quay "A la Harpe Couronnée," whose landlord was a certain Thomas Martin, whose establishment frequented by sailors had a bad reputation. At Dinan, another Irish "patron," MacDonagh, was well known. But perhaps the most famous of all the Irish bars was that kept by Margaret Collins, "A la Belle-Anglaise" (a rather unfortunate name!), in the Rue des Marins at Saint-Malo. In the reign of Louis XV there were some fifty *débits* in Saint-Malo patronized by sailors, exclusive of the most luxurious *hôtelleries* favoured by the well-to-do sea-captains and officers.

But to return to the present time. There is no organization which has done more to promote the moral, social, and physical welfare of the Breton sailor than the "Abris du Marin" founded by Monsieur J. de Thézac in 1898. It now owns and controls well-equipped fishermen's institutes at the following ports: Roscoff, Camaret, Douarnenez, Audierne, Ile-de-Sein, Guilvinec, Ile-Tudy, Sainte-Marine, Passage-Lanriec, Concarneau, Le Palais. These establishments provide not only clubs for the fishermen, but are centres for serious study, instruction being given in navigation, the use of motors, wireless telegraphy, and other matters connected with the everyday work of a modern fisherman. Some of the institutes have sleeping accommodation for sailors, some of them workshops for repairing boats, others well-equipped hospital accommodation where first aid can be given. In 1907 the French Academy awarded their highest Prix de Vertu to the "Abris du Marin." Every year their energetic founder, who still directs almost single-handed the working of this society, edits and publishes the *Almanach du Marin Breton*, which is enormously popular with the fisherman. It provides him with reading matter that is amusing as well as useful. The almanac is a unique volume. I know of nothing quite like it in the whole range of nautical literature, for it somehow manages to combine the character of a Nautical Almanac, a medical dictionary, a popular encyclopædia, with that of a comic Christmas annual! There can be few men who understand so thoroughly the complex temperament of the Breton sailor as Monsieur de Thézac. He has devoted his whole life to them. He is admired, respected, and loved by sailors of all ranks and ages. Very wisely he made it a rule when he began his work thirty years ago that no direct religious propaganda of any sort was allowed in his *abris*, otherwise the Socialists and Communists would never have set foot in them, so great was, and is still to a lesser degree, their hatred of anything even remotely connected with the Church. This attitude of complete external neutrality has meant that his work has been looked upon with a certain suspicion by most of the local priests and has lacked their support. But Monsieur de Thézac understands the mentality of his Breton fishermen, he

realizes that a large proportion of them have quite lost touch with
any sort of organized religion and are outside its moral as well
as its spiritual influence.   Their ingrained suspicion and prejudices
have to be overcome, and he feels that this can only be done by
an intelligent lay apostolate working on a much broader basis
than is conceived possible by the average seminary-trained priest.
It is not for me to say if he is right.   One can merely point to the
influence of his "Abris du Marin" and note that so far the Church
has not managed to get into touch with or to win back the class
of men whom one finds in these institutes where every one is welcome,
no matter if he be the most violent Socialist or red-hot Communist.
Each "Abri du Marin" has very much the same character.   You
enter the door and are confronted with a barometer which is
always being tapped and studied by the fishermen; notices are
pinned up on the wall concerning boats or motor-engines for sale,
changes of buoyage or lighting around the coasts.   Then you find
yourself in a large *salle de réunion*, somewhat suggestive of a school
classroom with its rows of benches and forms, and cupboards and
pictures everywhere on the walls: pictures and photographs, most
of them taken by Monsieur de Thézac himself, representing local
groups of fishermen, boats, men who have been saved from drowning,
regattas, village Pardons.   "Honneur et Patrie," "La porte du
cabaret conduit à l'hôpital," "La crainte de l'air est le commence-
ment de la tuberculose," "Eau de vie pour le marchand, mais
'ôte vie' pour le client," "La France est notre mère: travaillons
pour elle" and other like maxims of a moral character are displayed,
and add to the decoration of the room.   Upstairs you will find a
well-stocked library of well-thumbed books and magazines.   In
some of the institutes there is a gymnasium.   No alcoholic drink is
served for Monsieur de Thézac knows as well as any one how great
are the ravages being made on his countrymen in this direction,
and he is almost alone in attacking the evil in a practical manner.
His *abris* provide just that atmosphere of comradeship and cheerfulness that is otherwise only to be found in the café and *débit*, that
craving for something that will enable a man to forget the hardship
of his daily toil.   For this is the *raison d'être* of the drunkenness of

DOUARNENEZ
(Looking towards the "Abris du Marin")

the Breton fisherman, a natural instinct that has been perverted and that seeks the wrong outlet for its expression.

To see the *abris* at their best you must visit them in winter when the fishing fleets are in harbour. After the day is over and the night has closed in, their rooms are crowded with fishermen of all ages, white-haired veterans are mixed up with cheeky little *mousses*. It is often difficult to force one's way through the packed mass of seafaring humanity, especially if there is a lecture or conference to be given on some interesting subject, for these men are like children in their avidity to "listen to a story." The hurried traveller or tourist seldom gets the chance to get at the hearts and minds of these fishermen of rough exterior. They are so suspicious of strangers that it is long before they will venture to reveal anything of their inmost feelings. The hardships of their lives can only be fully appreciated when one has talked to them in the friendly atmosphere of one of these *abris*. Here the soul of maritime Brittany is shown to one as nowhere else. You may be lucky enough to assist at a concert, when you will hear some of those pathetic old Breton songs, with their note of mournful sadness, that harmonize so well with the windy, rain-swept landscape, like the ocean breaking on the rocky shores. Upstairs you will find groups of young men studying hard at navigation, or some other subject they need for their profession. Others will be reading, generally something to amuse, for the naturally melancholy Breton does not wish to hear anything more of the tragedies of life of which he knows far too much already. So if you peep over his shoulder you will probably find the sixteen- or seventeen-year-old *mousse* deep in Hans Andersen or Perrault, for fairy stories have an extraordinary popularity. More than one boy admits he takes a book of fairy stories to sea with him!

Such is the sort of work being carried on by the "Abris du Marin," and which might be extended to many other ports in Brittany if the necessary funds were forthcoming. The seamen themselves would support the work if it were started in their midst.

No book on maritime Brittany would be complete without some reference to the *syndicats*, or seamen's unions, which have such a

wide-spreading influence in every port along the coast.   But owing
to religious and political difficulties which do not exist in quite the
same way in Great Britain, the words "Labour" and "Socialism"
having an entirely different meaning in France to what they do
over here, these *syndicats* possess a very much more political character
than, for instance, has the National Union of Seamen with us.   For
a seaman to belong to a *syndicat* practically means that he is bound to
the political opinions that colour the programme of the *syndicat*.
Strange as it may seem in a country which is supposed to be predominantly Catholic, it was only last year that the first definitely
Catholic *syndicat* for seamen was founded in Brittany; until then every
Catholic seaman or fisherman was almost bound to belong to a
union which was passively, if not more often definitely, extreme
socialist or communist in the fullest "continental" signification.
I do not possess either the knowledge or the qualifications to criticize
the multifarious activities of these organizations.   But they must at
least be given the credit for having done their best to improve the
material and social conditions of the Breton fishermen and to have
defended and supported their interests against the often unjust
demands of shipowners and curers.   Without them the material
situation of the Breton fisherman might have been the same (or even
worse) to-day as it was fifty years ago.

NOTE. For further information regarding the activities of the socialist Fédéra-
tion Nationale des Syndicats Maritimes, refer to their official organ, *Le Travailleur
de la Mer*. For the Syndicats Chrétiens now being organized, see the publications
of the Confédération Française des Travailleurs Chrétiens.

CHAPTER III

THE Breton loves the sea, yet at the same time he fears it. He would like to forget the sea, but he cannot. The sea is always with him. He is never far enough away from it to escape its mysterious influence. He thinks of it as a brooding presence. At certain moments this undefined, elemental creature becomes a living personality, to be wooed or propitiated as the case may be.

God created the land. The devil made the sea. Such is the quasi-Manichæan belief of many a Breton sailor if you can get him to reveal his inmost feelings to you. And this is not easy unless his shyness and reserve have been broken down with the aid of alcohol!

Hence arises a perpetual conflict of emotions in his life. He is always afraid of the sea in one sense, yet in another there is no braver seaman to be found anywhere else in the world. An eternal conflict and strife of feeling and imagination against the stern necessities of life.

"How was the sea created?" you ask the Breton fisherman. "Was there always a sea?" The Breton sailor, the older generation at least, whose life was not so complex and less of a sordid rush than it is to-day, had many theories of the origin of the world which are not those of the author of the Book of Genesis. He was a pious Catholic, of course, but his theology was often heterodox. He could not read, and he found his explanation of the mysteries of life rather in the old legends handed down from generation to generation, than in the teaching of the Church Catechism. Nowadays belief in these old legends has been almost destroyed, owing to the so-called scientific instruction given in the *écoles laïques*. You will not find many Breton seamen at the present moment who will tell you that God created the sea with a bucket of water and three grains of salt. Yet a hundred years ago most of the Saint-Malo fisherfolk believed this![1]

[1] Cf. W. Branch Johnson, *Folk Tales of Brittany*.

In some of those picturesque little villages on the estuary of the Rance, below Dinan, it is possible that you might still find some of the old folk who remember the legend that after the deluge the earth became so dry and parched up that the *bon Dieu* told the birds of the air to fly to Paradise, and return each one of them with a drop of water in his beak. That is how the ocean began, they would tell you!

Going farther west along the coast, there may yet be some of the older generation of fishermen at Binic who remember the tale how God, Saint Peter, and Saint John, happening to pay a visit to Brittany one Wednesday, found nobody willing to give them hospitality, because the king who then ruled over the country had made a law that no water was to be drawn between Tuesday and Saturday, for at that time there was a drought in the land. They were getting tired and thirsty. The weather was hot. At last they came to a cottage where an old woman said she would give them to eat and drink. So they sat down and refreshed themselves. But the old woman would not take anything in payment. Whereupon the *bon Dieu* said to Saint Peter: "Give her that barrel you are carrying under your arm, and tell her if she turns on the tap and wishes, anything she desires will be granted her." The heavenly visitors having departed, the old woman, realizing that they had drunk up all her water and that she could not draw any more until Saturday, turned on the tap of the barrel and wished. Water began to trickle out, then to flow rapidly. She filled every bucket and pail she had in the house and still the water flowed. Suddenly she remembered that she had not asked how to stop the supply. The water still went on flowing until at last it flooded the house, the village, and all the surrounding country . . . and it is still flowing to-day. That is one explanation of the origin of the sea, which will never dry up until the barrel stops flowing at the last day.[1]

A pretty legend! Here is another of a different character which comes from Saint-Briac, also quoted by the same author.

The sun got jealous of the earth many hundreds of years ago

[1] op. cit.

and tried to burn it up. So the pious folk prayed hard to God to help them. The Almighty, feeling sorry for the poor people on the earth, told all His saints who were in Paradise to command the sun to go back to where he belonged. But the sun paid no attention and went on blazing away nearer and nearer to the earth. The saints first tried persuasion, then threats, to no purpose. Ordinary weapons were useless when dealing with an enemy like the sun. Suddenly one of the saints (the legend does not relate who it was) had an inspiration . . . had not the *bon Dieu* provided him and his brethren with certain natural functions that would serve their purpose admirably? So forthwith they took aim and attacked the sun with such violence, continuing without ceasing for more than eight days. The sun had to retreat. He could not resist such a deluge. Since then he has kept away from the earth. And that is one explanation of the origin of the sea and why it is salt.

Many and curious are the beliefs still held on some parts of the coast of Brittany as to the origin of the waves. Around Saint-Malo one comes across the tradition that the sorcerer already referred to jumps into the sea from time to time in order to find his magic mill . . . it is the movement made by his swimming that produces the waves.

Thousands of years ago, so it is said, there was no wind in this part of the globe, the sea was always dead calm, and sailors had always to row everywhere. A certain captain having heard that there was a country far off where the winds lived, he determined to find his way thither and take them captive. So for many months his crew rowed on and on until at last they came to the country of the winds. After much trouble the captain managed to take the winds prisoner. He sewed them up in sacks and stowed them away in the hold of his ship and started to row home. His idea was to drown the bad winds and set free the good ones. But one of the sailors was curious to see what was inside the sacks. He took out his knife, made a hole in one of them, and out rushed the wind. To make matters worse it was one of the bad winds, the fierce "Suroît" that blows from the south-west. A gale

Le Légué, Saint-Brieuc

sprang up suddenly. The ship was swamped and sank, and the crew were drowned. All the other winds, both good and bad, escaped from their sacks. Ever since they have been wandering around the world as a danger to seafarers.[1]

In all maritime countries you come across legends concerning the origin of tides. Brittany is no exception. In some places you are told that tides are caused by the breathing of a great monster which comes up to the surface of the water from time to time for air. There are villages in La Basse-Bretagne where the old people say that a rising tide is full of poisons that are deposited on the beach. They believe that all sorts of human events are connected with the tides in some mysterious manner. In some places there is a belief that children are always born on the ebb tide, in other places it is maintained that births only occur during a flood tide. Elsewhere they will tell you that a woman will bring forth a boy if childbirth takes place when the tide is rising, a girl if it is flowing. No hope can be had when a sick man gets worse as the tide is going out, for deaths always occur during the ebb. As a general rule you may take it that it is better not to kill pigs except when the tide is going out; your bacon will taste better. But on other parts of the coast of Brittany you will be told that hogs should be killed with the incoming tide, sows when it is ebbing. At Concarneau they used to say that the tide would always go back to allow the Blessed Sacrament to be carried round the town. At Ploumanac'h, near Perros-Guirec, it was held that the tide would always recede to enable pilgrims to approach the shrine of Saint Guirec on the day of his Pardon. It is in no way contrary to pious Catholic tradition to believe that the angels, especially Saint Michael, have been given certain special powers over inanimate nature. Pilgrims to Mont Saint-Michel were always sure that the archangel would never allow them to be drowned by the incoming tides which flow up so suddenly around that famous rock.

Never get your hair cut when the tide is coming in, otherwise you are sure to catch cold. When the tide is rising never make mattresses or eiderdowns of the feathers of sea-birds or they will

[1] op. cit.

PERROS-GUIREC

swell and burst, and be sure to sow clover when the tide is on the flood, or the cows which eat it will also burst. Perhaps you do not know what a great risk you run by taking a bath when the tide is coming in? It will bring about disaster in some form or other sooner or later. If you notice what a good taste the butter you are eating at breakfast has, then you may be sure it was made when the tide was on the ebb.

Such are but a few typical examples of legends concerning the sea, the waves and the tides, and their influence on human beings, that are to be found everywhere on the coast of Brittany.

Superstitious practices play such an important part in the every-day life of the Breton mariners that the only way in which one can study them methodically is to arrange them in some sort of chrono-logical order, beginning with the birth of a child and ending with the death of an old man.

Throughout maritime Brittany there would seem to be a general idea that the wife of a sailor has a more painful childbirth when her husband is at sea. At Saint-Cast there is an old superstition that there will be calm weather for the rest of the day if a fisherman's son has been born on a rising tide. A male child used always to be placed in a fisherman's basket almost immediately after birth in order that he should become a good fisherman later on. His cradle would be covered with a sailor's jersey: a charm against contracting dangerous illnesses. Down in the "sailor town" of Légué, below Saint-Brieuc, they used to say that a boy born on a rising tide at Christmas was sure to become a sea captain:

> A mer montante de Noël,
> Garçon qui naît devient capitaine.

At Saint-Malo, mothers would put shells in their babies' cradles so that they might follow the sea later on. When a year or two old, the baby boy in the fisher homes was never jogged up and down on his mother's knee to suggest riding on horseback. There was no "Ride-a-cock-horse to Banbury Cross," or similar infant games, but an early initiation into the actions of swimming or the movements of a boat at sea:

> Nage à sec, ou nage à terre,

the Breton fisherwife would sing, pretending to teach her little boy to swim.

On the Ile-de-Sein horses are unknown, and here the infant in arms is amused by his father or mother by the recital of some Breton verse, accompanied by appropriate actions.

Paul Sébillot tells us how the old "Terre-Neuvas" sailor when he was ashore would amuse his little children by pretending to catch fish, imitating the actions of a fisherman hauling in the cod. At Saint-Malo, parents would take the tiny fists of children in their hands, making them catch hold of an imaginary oar, meanwhile singing some slow rhythmic chant. And as soon as his little son was old enough to understand the meaning of words, the father would talk to him of boats, and ships, and fishing. Almost his earliest toys were shell-fish and crabs. What fun he would get pulling off their legs!

In many places, around Cap Fréhel for instance, it was the custom on Christmas Eve for the fishermen to go out on the rocks at low tide and gather seaweed. When cutting it they would recite a certain prayer or incantation, and on their return home part of the strange ritual to be observed involved walking on their hands and feet! On Christmas morning the seaweed was boiled in water and given to the children to drink, but before doing so they had to spit on the seaweed and make the sign of the cross. It was firmly believed that this drink sharpened their wits and gave them the power of working hard. The explanation of this curious ceremonial being based on the tradition that the Infant Jesus had bestowed on the seaweed certain peculiar properties that never failed to produce results on all children who drank an infusion made from them![1]

A few years later and the future mariner of Brittany has grown into a strong, healthy boy, full of robust high spirits and mischievousness. His anxious mother is afraid her child will come to some harm if he goes wandering about on the rocks or clambering about in the boats. So she tries to frighten him by saying that terrible monsters are waiting there to eat up little boys. For instance,

[1] Sébillot, *Archivio*, vol. v, p. 519.

there is "le gros Nicole," and "le gros Jean." The former seizes hold of children and shuts them up in a cask where they will have nothing to eat but seaweed and only salt water to drink. As to the other, he has claws like a great lobster with which he scratches and tears at the faces of the little fisher-boys whom he finds playing about on the beach.[1]

The mothers of Saint-Cast threaten another alarming punishment in store for their disobedient children if they won't do as they are told, i.e. to be taken out to the farthest end of the "Ile," where fairies will beat them with the long ribbon-like tails of seaweed.[2]

As in seaport towns and villages all the world over, so too in Brittany, you will find the boys playing with toy boats or fishing almost as soon as they can walk. With other boys of their own age they will organize miniature regattas. Sometimes, with a mischievousness that is not so common in this country, you find them putting beetles and other insects on their toy boats, watching their futile efforts to escape being drowned with wild excitement and glee. In winter time, when the constant rain and driving winds often prevent them from playing outdoors, these future seamen amuse themselves at home, with an upturned table acting as a ship, one boy pretending to steer, others fishing or rowing. Even to-day in most of the fishing villages parents make their children go barefoot in summer so as to accustom them to life on board ship later on.

In the days before modern ideas of prudery had invaded the coasts of Brittany, and contact with visitors and tourists had introduced more "civilized" customs, you would find the fisher children rolling themselves naked in the sand before they ran into the sea to bathe. It was supposed that this bath of sand was good for the health. Before entering the water they never failed to make the sign of the cross, because, as they said, if they were drowned they would then go to heaven.[3] The same custom is found in other Catholic countries, notably in Portugal.

I have been unable to discover any traces of rites of initiation among the seafarers of Brittany, except the following, which is

---

[1] Sébillot, *Revue des Traditions Populaires*, vol. i, p. 7.
[2] Sébillot, *Archivio*, vol. v, p. 518.
[3] Sébillot, *Revue des Traditions Populaires*, vol. ii.

The Quays and Sardine Boats, Audierne

described by Monsieur H. le Carguet (*Revue des Traditions Populaires,* vol. xiv, p. 613), but I have no doubt that they used to exist, as in all other maritime communities.

At Audierne, he writes, the boys are enrolled as *mousses* on the fishing-boats soon after the age of nine. (This would be impossible to-day owing to compulsory education till a later age.) A father would say to his son one evening: "Demain tu iras boëtter; je t'ai mis au rôle . . . puis tu seras baptisé." The rite of initiation was known as the "Baptême du Mousse." It was always a proud moment for any boy even if he feared the brutal and coarse treatment at which his elder brothers and companions had often hinted. The following morning he goes down to the bed of the river at low tide where he is met by his companions. They welcome him heartily, offer him their tobacco, their cigarette papers, and produce bottles of wine and brandy from which they force him to drink. Before very long the lad is more or less drunk. Seeing him in this condition they start singing "Plijadur an den meo" (*Plaisirs de l'homme saoul*), a parody of an old Breton song which describes the joys of Paradise. The first part of the ceremony being over, the *mousses* next proceed to "baptize" their new member.

They surround the dazed lad, tell him to undress, and if he hesitates strip him naked by force. Then the ceremony begins. Some of the elder boys gathering up handfuls of gravel rub it all over the body of their victim. Others proceed to cover his genital organs with lumps of mud and slime. They continue this coarse and brutal treatment so roughly that sometimes the victim faints, or collapses in a drunken stupor. The *mousses* then decide on what name they will give their new companion. These names ("tee names" they are called in Scotland) generally refer to some peculiarity of the newly "baptized," or else bear some relation to his father's career at sea. When the ceremony is over the neophyte's body is cleaned and washed. He is helped to dress and escorted back to his home to the accompaniment of songs which refer to the nature of the act in which he has just taken part. The proud father eagerly inquires what name his son has been given; the mother looks on sadly, realizing that her boy has no longer the same need of her as hitherto.

Cases have been known in which the victims never recovered from the brutal treatment of these rites of initiation. Most of the older seafarers on the coast of Brittany admit they have taken part in similar ceremonies, but not always of such a coarse and savage character as that I have just described. Often the rite of initiation consists of no more than burying the naked victim in the sand up to his waist.

On the north coast of Brittany no boat was ever laid down until her health had been drunk in the boat-builder's yard. "On arrose le bateau," they would say. As soon as the hull was completed it was given a sort of preliminary christening: the shipwrights sprinkled it with salt water, reciting appropriate words. When the moment arrived to launch the fishing-boat, the shipwright would take up the chant, and, the vessel being afloat, a sail would be hung over each side while more verses were recited.

The mariners of Brittany were no exception to those of all other Catholic countries in believing that a vessel that had not been blessed would be sure to come to some bad end. Sébillot relates that at Saint-Cast in the year 1880 a certain fisherman was catching no fish and pretended that it was due to the fact that his boat had never been blessed by the priest.

The older generation of Breton fishermen were convinced that if the "patron" of a vessel had not been baptized he was sure to be drowned. On the south coast many of the sailors still believe that a ship which has "not been made a Christian" has no luck, and it is almost impossible to find a crew for her.

Many and curious are the actual ceremonies connected with the baptism of a fishing vessel. On the Côtes-du-Nord, the ceremony generally takes place three days after the arrival of the vessel in the port to which she belongs. Often, for the sake of greater solemnity, the function is arranged for a Sunday. The vessel is decorated with flags and lanterns. A name is given her, the priest recites the liturgical prayers prescribed in the *Rituale* and sprinkles her with holy water; during which rites one of the fishermen will distribute *pain bénit* to all those who are on board, just as if they were in church. Several packets of biscuits are crushed on the deck and then the "patron" smashes a bottle of wine against the bows. The "godfather" and "godmother" then go up on to the deck, pick up the remains of the biscuits, and drink what is left of the wine. The godfather of the vessel is called her *compère de bois*, the other is the *commère*—both having named a "creature of wood" and not a human being. The ceremony being over, everybody leaves the ship. When they are ashore, a rope is tied round the "patron" and he is led home by his wife as if he were a sheep! He is not supposed to have anything to eat that night, and has to go to bed supperless.[1]

At Plouëzec, a large village three miles south-east of Paimpol, most of whose male inhabitants are engaged in the Newfoundland cod fisheries, the ceremonies accompanying the christening of a ship are even more elaborate. The priest blesses large, round, flat cakes made without sugar, which are later on distributed to those present. Assisted by the sacristan and choir the priest chants the *Te Deum*, and then proceeds to bless the vessel. The "god-father" and "godmother" each in turn give several blows with a hammer on five small bolts or pins, into the holes of which has been previously placed some *pain bénit*. These pins are arranged in the shape of a cross. The religious ceremony concludes with the singing of the *Ave Maris Stella*, the *parrain* and *marraine* distributing pieces of cake and *dragées* to all the onlookers.

In his *Folk-Lore des Pêcheurs*, p. 146, Sébillot states that when a ship sails on her first voyage from Saint-Malo she is always the last to leave the port. The sailor who catches the first fish is given a bottle of wine. Half the contents of the bottle are poured into the belly of the fish, which is then thrown back into the sea, because, so the fishermen say, the other fish will smell the wine and swim near the ship in the hope of getting more. The same authority informs us that if a vessel is damaged on taking the water for the first time, she is brought back to port and not allowed to sail again for a week.

Some strange superstitions are to be found in relation to the manner of discovering whether fishing will be good or bad. In

---

[1] Sébillot, *Folk-Lore des Pêcheurs*, pp. 142–3.

Le Palais, Belle-Ile

La Basse-Bretagne if the wind blows from the west during the Gospel of the Mass on Palm Sunday, it is an infallible sign that the next herring season will be a bad one. On the other hand, a north or south-east wind is regarded as propitious.[1]

A curious superstition prevalent on the coast of Finistère and Morbihan, is that the sardines have a king known as *le Maigre*. When he comes across a shoal of his subjects, he devours the lot, making a bank higher than a mountain, which may be seen projecting out of the water.[2]

The presence of certain birds at particular seasons is also supposed to affect the luck of a fisherman. For instance, at Saint-Jacut-de-la-Mer the cuckoo is said to be very fond of skate. The first boat to see or hear this bird would throw overboard a fish as an offering, believing that this would bring good luck during the summer fishing season. Herpin, in the *Revue des Traditions Populaires* (vol. xiii, p. 98), relates that in one of the little fishing villages on Belle-Ile there used to be a chapel dedicated to Saint Joseph, which the sailors always visited on returning home after fishing. One day a benefactor presented a statue of Saint Peter to this chapel and removed Saint Joseph to a cave at the other end of the island. Soon afterwards, a fisherman entering the chapel beheld to his astonishment, not the statue, but Saint Joseph in person, and at his side a beautiful lady dressed in white, no doubt the Blessed Virgin, who was trying to console him. It would seem that her efforts were in vain, because the fisherman stated that poor Saint Joseph shed a tear so large that it trickled away into the sea. It was so salt a tear that it drove away all the sardines from that part of the coast, and they had to wait many years before they came back again.

In the year 1886, the villagers of Sauzon, on Belle-Ile, were convinced that the dearth of sardines was directly due to the Republican Government! Owing to this "*sacrée*" *république*, they protested, one could catch nothing but mackerel in the Coureau de Groix.[3]

Like fishermen all the world over those of Brittany attach great

---

[1] G. de la Landelle, *Mœurs maritimes*, p. 143.
[2] Cambry, *Voyage dans le Finistère*, p. 335. [3] *Le Temps*, 23rd April, 1886.

importance to certain days of the month in connection with their luck at sea. Until a few years ago, the Breton sailors were as careful to abstain from fishing on Sundays as are their brethren in Scotland even to-day. There is a story told at Saint-Cast how the Blessed Virgin appeared in person to reproach some local fishermen who had gone to sea on a Sunday. They paid no attention to her warnings, with the result that, soon after, many vessels were wrecked, and the Banq-de-la-Horaine, where formerly fish were plentiful, was deserted.[1]

Strange stories have come down to us of what happened to fishermen who put to sea on holy-days of obligation. In one case the wife of a man who had violated the rule of the Church gave birth to a son who had a head like a fish! At Paimpol there is related a story of a boat that went fishing on Good Friday, and instead of fish dragged up crosses.[2] The sailors of Saint-Cast were convinced that if they dared to fish on Easter Day, porpoises would come in near shore and drive away all the mackerel. One Ascension Day some fishermen of Saint-Cast, who had put to sea despite the warnings of the *curé*, were terrified by the sudden appearance of the dreaded "sea devil" known as "Nicole."

In these days the faith and credulity of the Breton fisherman is not what it was fifty years ago. He is still more or less superstitious, and takes care to observe the ancient taboos when possible, but in most fishing centres all round the coast he has ceased to pay any attention to the laws of the Church to which his grandfathers were so faithful. It is not for me to say whether he is any better seaman or fisherman in consequence of a less superstitious and childlike belief in the efficacy of the supernatural.

In all fishing communities it is the duty of one of the crew to go round to the houses of the others and wake up his shipmates by knocking at their doors to warn them it is time to embark. Sébillot tells us that at Saint-Cast it was the custom to awaken the men with some popular verse. In the same village, the fishermen always make it a sort of sacramental rite to *boire la goutte* (i.e. take a drink of brandy) before hoisting their sails, maintaining

---

[1] Sébillot, *Légendes Locales*, vol. i, pp. 8, 38.   [2] Sébillot, *Folk-Lore*, p. 165.

that the fish were attracted by the smell of the brandy. In like manner they always demanded a bottle of brandy when they had landed an exceptionally good catch.

Among the *Terre-Neuvas* existed the almost universal custom of consulting the *os de vérité*, as they called it. In codfish there are two bones near the gills which resemble the blades of a knife. The sailors used to throw them into the air without looking at them, taking care that the "bone of truth" did not touch any other object before falling on the deck. At the same time the man would invoke the fetish in the following manner: "If you do not tell me that I shall to-day catch (ten, twenty) fish, I am going to smash you with my knife." If the *os de vérité* fell on the deck with the two ends downwards, it meant a negative answer. If, on the contrary, they were uppermost, with the middle part lying down on the ground, that signified "yes." If the bone replied "no," then it was kicked with the man's boot, and interrogated anew. On the terre-neuvas and in ports of northern Brittany men used to keep their *os de vérité* for several months, and often consulted them; its advice was asked in every sort of difficulty. In a similar manner the two little head-bones of the skate were used as oracles.[1]

Just as on the east coast of Scotland, so too in Brittany, fishermen do not like to be asked where they propose to fish. It is supposed to bring bad luck, especially when the interrogator is a woman.

In a like manner it is thought to bring bad luck if anybody stares hard at a sailor before he embarks. The fishermen around Tréguier were convinced that it was useless to go to sea if they met a tailor on the way to their boats. Some of them, however, maintained that the "charm" of his evil eye could be removed if one immediately said a prayer to the Blessed Virgin. On the coast of Morbihan this superstition was even more definite. One could not even mention the name of a tailor, for it was sure to bring bad luck.

A still more curious superstition was to be found at Paimpol, where if a fisherman chanced to meet a *dévote* (i.e. a woman well known for her piety) he would return home, take holy water,

---

[1] Sébillot, *Traditions et Superstitions*, vol. ii, pp. 263-4, 269.

recite a *Pater* and an *Ave*, and make the sign of the cross before he ventured to embark.[1]

With slight differences, this belief was held all along the north coast of Brittany. Cats were also held to be unlucky to meet on one's way to the harbour, and this superstition seems to exist in many other parts of Europe. Strange to say, meeting a horse or an ass is looked upon as very lucky. Breton fishermen have the same dread of mentioning the word "rabbit" as their Scottish brethren have of the word "salmon." In most of the Breton ports it is generally believed that it is unlucky to have a cat on board a fishing-boat.

An extraordinary superstition is said to have prevailed at Audierne, that if a crew wanted to be sure of a good catch one of their number must sleep with the wife of the skipper on the eve of putting to sea at the beginning of the season!

Sébillot affirms that the fishermen of Saint-Malo were convinced that it was always better never to keep a boat too clean, otherwise fish would not bite. On the Newfoundland Banks a similar belief prevailed, the crews maintaining that the smell of the offal on the decks attracted other fish![2] The presence on board of certain dead animals was looked upon as lucky, e.g. a *minard*.

The slightest theft committed on a vessel was (quite rightly!) supposed to bring about misfortune, even jealousy between families.[3] In Finistère, when a theft had been committed on board a fishing vessel, the crew were accustomed to burn damp straw in the hold, so as to drive out the evil spirit of the robber who was supposed to be hiding there. But as the evil spirit was capable of making himself very small, it was essential that the smoke should penetrate into every tiny crack. Only after this fumigation was it worth while for a fishing vessel to put to sea.[4]

At Audierne, where so many superstitions existed, all sorts of curious methods were employed to get rid of an evil spirit which had taken up his abode on board. One of them is to steal some

---

[1] Sébillot, *Folk-Lore des Pêcheurs*, p. 183.
[2] *Traditions Populaires*, vol. ii, p. 247.
[3] Cf. G. de la Landelle, *Mœurs Maritimes*.
[4] G. de la Landelle, *Mœurs Maritimes*.

object from another boat alongside! This done, the evil spirit, *le Bosj*, will leave the vessel and jump on board the other.

Another method was to "beat" the *Bosj*. A handful of oat straw had to be stolen and taken on board the boat without any one noticing it. At night, when they were at sea, and the rest of the crew were asleep, the straw would be set alight at the foot of the mast by one of the men, to the cry of "The devil is on board." The sailors, awakened by the smell of smoke, jump up and knock everything about. The *Bosj*, stifled by the smoke, burnt by the fire, hunted down, beaten on all sides, jumps into the sea![1]

The same authority states that on the Ile-de-Sein, in order to dispel bad luck, the fishermen steal some nets, burn its corks, break a plate, and put the pieces instead of bait in the lobster-pots, and scrape and put in the fire the bark of the wooden rings of which the pots are made.

To drive away evil spirits the women of the Pointe du Raz often make their husbands wear a *louzou* or magic bag, which preserves them from the evil eye and brings them luck when fishing.[2]

Monsieur Le Carguet also writes that a certain Pobet-Coz, an old fisherman of Audierne who wore one of these *louzou* stitched into his jumper, was so lucky at sea that they used to say of him: "Pobet with the nails catches more fish than the Audiernais with their hooks. This luck will last so long as his jumper keeps its *louzou*." One day the bag fell out of a hole in the lining, and the *mousse* in ignorance threw it overboard. From that moment poor Pobet-Coz had no better luck than any other fisherman of Audierne.

Breton fishermen share the same superstitions regarding priests as sailors all the world over; likewise the same dread of referring to hares and rabbits when they are at sea. Even worse is it to mention the word "wolf." Should this fatal word be uttered on board any one of the older generation of fishermen would immediately return to harbour.

A more recent custom is for the "patron" to throw back into the water the first fish caught, saying these words: "Tiens,'ki-coat,"

---

[1] H. le Carguet, *Revue des Traditions Populaires*, vol. iv, p. 537.
[2] H. le Carguet, *Revue des Traditions Populaires*, vol. iv, p. 467.

LIGHTHOUSE, ILE-DE-SEIN

(wooden dog, i.e. wolf), "that's where you belong." In this way the charm is broken.[1]

Having arrived at their fishing-grounds, the Breton fishermen used to invoke the sea, the birds, or often the fish itself in some curious formula. Off the Newfoundland Banks the *Terre-Neuvas* would drive away the skate in a similar manner.

Off the Côtes-du-Nord, sea-birds would be frightened away from frightening the fish by other charms.

In many parts of the world crabs are regarded as evil spirits by sailors: the Bretons are no exception to this belief. If they met them on the shore, they would crush them.

On many parts of the coast of Brittany the fishermen used always to address the fish in doggerel verse before shooting their nets or casting their lines. Sébillot (*Folk-Lore des Pêcheurs*, pp. 239–43) gives many examples of these formulæ. They also made use of certain prayers to Our Lady and the saints, also cast in verse form.

The sailors of Morbihan were accustomed to observe the following ritual when they were fishing for sardine: The "patron" would take out a bottle of holy water stowed away in the stern of the boat and pass it to the man who was stationed in the bow. Having uncorked it, he would sprinkle his fingers with the water and then pass the bottle to his neighbour. Each member of the crew did the same, all keeping strict silence. The skipper received it last. Then they all stood up, made the sign of the cross, and proceeded to arrange their nets. This done, the skipper would sprinkle them with holy water, first from stern to bow, then across, reciting at the same time some appropriate prayer, often improvised.[2] On their return from fishing it was the custom, in certain parts of Brittany, for the crews to sing songs if they had done well. Monsieur Herpin, in his *La Côte d'Émeraude*, says that at Cancale after a good catch of oysters the fishermen used to dance on the decks on their "bisquines." On the coast of Finistère, the boat which brought back the first haul of sardines at the beginning of the season used to be decorated with flowers. I am told that the first sample of

[1] Le Carguet, op. cit., p. 536.
[2] G. de la Landelle, *Mœurs Maritimes*, p. 138.

sardine to be landed is still called *le bouquet*, a relic of this custom.[1]

In another chapter I have described the daily life of the *Terre-Neuvas*, or Newfoundland cod fishermen, and many of the curious customs and superstitions still observed on board their "goëlettes," so I will not repeat them here.

There are stories, too, of captains of "terre-neuvas" who gave themselves up to the devil or who committed grave sins in order to have luck at fishing. The captain of the *Saint-Marcan* having done very badly for some time exclaimed one day: "I would gladly sell my soul if only I could catch a fish." Soon afterwards his luck changed, but later on his ship was lost in a tempest. At Saint-Cast a tale is related of a certain captain who made a similar contract, catching plenty of fish, after which the devil himself towed his ship back to Saint-Malo in four days.[2]

In the *Revue des Traditions Populaires* (vol. xii, p. 392) the story is told how the captain of a "terre-neuvas," finding his ship becalmed, went down into the cabin and started to abuse the image of Our Lady, asking her if she were the cause of all this bad weather. He gave the image a blow with his fist, and it rolled on to the deck, smashed into several pieces. Soon after a breeze arose, the vessel was damaged, the captain was drowned, and the crew caught hardly any cod. The men were convinced that this was due to their captain and that his soul was damned. Some of them said they had seen him skimming over the waves in the form of a burning fire, and that the moment a fish was on the line they felt an invisible hand which let it go free again.

In other parts of Europe the legendary stories of seafaring life, handed down orally from one generation to another, seldom refer to fairies and other supernatural beings as actually engaged in fishing. But in Brittany it was firmly believed that the *fées* and their husbands, *les féetauds*, went fishing—one of whom carried his boat under his arm when he was ashore, being able to enlarge its size when he embarked. Fairies were also credited with removing

---

[1] G. de la Landelle, *Mœurs Maritimes*, p. 138.
[2] *France Maritime*, vol. iii, p. 276.

oysters from the beds at Cancale, and replacing them with others of a better quality![1]

The sailors of Morbihan had some strange tales of a mysterious goldfish with a body as big as a calf. His head was like a gurnet, with horns, his body like that of a lobster, his tail like that of a swallow. If one was lucky enough to catch him, one would rip open his belly, put the gold in a sack, and then throw him back into the water.[2]

In his *Contes de Basse-Bretagne* Monsieur Luzel relates that once upon a time there was a fisherman who had no luck. He maintained that a sorceress had cast a spell upon him. One day he caught a mermaid, who promised, if she was thrown back into the sea, that she would drive into his nets as many fish as he desired. On two occasions this happened to the fisherman. The mermaid then told him that he would find on returning home that his wife had given birth to a fine boy, but that the fisherman must bring the baby out to sea with him, so that the mermaid could give him a kiss.

Another popular story told in the north coast of Brittany relates how a certain fisherman, who had thrown back into the sea the king of the fishes, was ordered by the ruler of the country to put out to sea again in order to secure this marvellous fish and bring him to the monarch, under pain of death. But the god of the sea gave the fisherman an enchanted boat, with which he conquered the royal fleet and eventually became king of France.

One might continue to quote hundreds more of similar tales, but the right environment in which to hear them is when they are told at sea in one of the stuffy little cabins on board some old wooden "goëlette" off the Newfoundland Banks, or on a cold winter's night around the fireside of a fisherman's cottage on the Côtes-du-Nord, or in one of the cosy little bars of the dark alleys of Saint-Malo or Paimpol, when they are filled with seamen, and the atmosphere is thick with clouds of tobacco-smoke, damp clothes, and the smell of rum and *eau-de-vie*. Only then can one fully

---

[1] Cf. Sébillot, *Contes des Marins*, p. 4; *Contes des Paysans et des Pêcheurs*, p. 65.
[2] Paul Féval, *Musée des Familles*, 1864, p. 254.

appreciate their naïve quality and the effect they produce on their listeners. Reproduced in print they often seem merely childish.

Superstitions and strange beliefs connected with death are as common in Brittany as in all Celtic countries. At Paimpol the wives of the Iceland fishermen who have been without news of their husbands for a longer time than usual, are accustomed to make a pilgrimage to Saint-Loup-le-Petit, between Plouëzec and Plouha, where they light a candle before the image of the saint in the chapel. If the flame burns brightly they take it as an omen that all is well. If the flame flickers and goes out, then they know that their husband is dead (Anatole Le Braz, op. cit., vol. i, p. 8). The same writer gives many examples of second sight among the fisherfolk of Brittany connected with the approach of death: sailors appearing to their wives and families; mysterious noises heard at night; strange dreams that come true; phantom ships visible after dark; all of them taken to be supernatural warnings of deaths that have recently occurred or that are soon to happen.

No matter where one goes along the coast, it is clear that the dreaded *ankou* is still believed in. The *ankou* is the personification of death itself, a belief common to many other countries besides Brittany. The last to die in any parish before the end of the year becomes the *ankou* for the following year. He is depicted as a tall and lean man with long white hair, his face overshadowed by a wide-brimmed felt hat. In some places he appears in the form of a skeleton shrouded in white, his head spinning round on his vertebral column like a top, so that he can embrace in one glance the whole region which he is visiting. He drags a cart after him. Sometimes he sits in this cart when it is harnessed to a team of scraggy horses. He is accompanied by two equally macabre companions, one of whom holds the bridle of the horses, the other runs on ahead and opens the gates of the fields, and knocks at the doors of houses where a death will take place during the following twelve months.

Fishermen tell of strange things they have seen which foretell the approach of some epidemic of illness or disease. Once a strange boat with black sails was seen off the Pointe du Raz.

Suddenly there rose out of it a cloud of smoke in the shape of a woman and drifted towards the land without touching the surface of the water. It was the plague. The following day it broke out in one of the villages near by and before long hundreds had died.

On the Ile-de-Sein it is said that certain women have *le don de vouer*, i.e. the power of communicating with the Evil One, and that on dark nights they have been seen by the fishermen embarking mysterious boats (*bag-sorcèrs*) in order to take part in the *groac'hed*, or "witches' sabbath." But these are things one does not talk about openly for it may lead to harm! If any one should have an enemy and wish to get rid of him on the quiet he can do so, by coming to an agreement with these women, the *voueuse* receiving a generous fee for her services. Once the matter has been arranged you need not worry; your enemy will disappear on the very day you have settled. The method employed is as follows: The *voueuse* must make three trips in the *bag-sorcèrs*, assist at three *groac'hed*, handing over each time to the demons of the wind and the sea some object belonging to the doomed man. And it is stated that on many occasions fishermen have mysteriously disappeared quite suddenly, and their friends are sure it is due to some satanic influence brought to bear by these women.[1]

Among the fisherfolk of Douarnenez, no funeral was complete without a copious repast served to the mourners towards the hour of midnight. It was believed that the dead man took part in this meal and a place was always laid for him. If this was not done, the departed one would not have the strength to survive the period of purgation that awaited him before arriving at eternal happiness. It is interesting to find that the same custom existed in the north of Scotland among the fishermen, also in Ireland.

Among the seafaring families on the Ile-de-Sein, not content with praying for the repose of the soul of the dead man whose body is actually present at these funeral watches, a *De Profundis* is recited for every member of the family whose name can be recalled. The old people have astonishing memories, and these prayers may sometimes be kept up for many hours on end. At one time it was

---

[1] Cf. *Folk Tales of Brittany*.

always the custom on the Ile-de-Sein for a fisherman who had lost his wife to ask her near relations to dig the grave, he himself giving the measurements. The work over, they repaired to the nearest *auberge* for a drink. The grave-diggers had always the privilege of carrying the coffin. Before leaving for the cemetery a saucepan of soup was set to boil. On the return of the funeral party this would be served out, accompanied by glasses of brandy.[1]

Here is another curious custom connected with the Ile-de-Sein. The fishermen of Loguivy, near Paimpol, who used to fish every summer off the island, if any of their number died away from home, had the custom of kissing the coffin before it left the church for the cemetery. Five years later the bones would be dug up and put on board a fishing-boat so that they could be reinterred at Loguivy, in the ossuary that is always found in every Breton graveyard.

Many and strange are the stories told of drowned men. At Gultraz, Ile-Saint-Gildas, off Port-Blanc, it is said that drowned seamen are often seen landing on the shore in search of fresh water. They walk up the beach in a long, silent procession with a woman at their head. Sometimes they are heard whispering to each other in low voices. But nothing has ever been made of its meaning, the only intelligible words being "ia . . . ia . . ." (yes, yes). And far out on the surface of the water their vessel is dimly visible as if lost in the clouds.[1]

When the fishermen of Trévou-Tréguignec, near Port-Blanc, embark at night they often see the hands of male corpses clinging on to the sides of their boats. The women do not venture so close, but let their hair float on the surface of the waves so that oars get entangled in it.[1]

A certain fisherman of Port-Blanc relates how one night he was walking along the beach in search of wreckage. His foot knocked against something that emitted a hollow sound and rolled away towards the edge of the water. After some searching he discovered, much to his disappointment, that it was nothing more valuable than a human skull. So he picked it up and chucked it away as far as possible. Suddenly a great wailing noise arose out on the

[1] Anatole Le Braz, op. cit., vol. i, p. 295 seq.

sea, and the horrified fisherman beheld thousands of arms rising out of the water. At the same time invisible hands tried to drag away the net he was carrying. He realized that he had done wrong in not showing greater respect for the head of this dead man. So he went back, and after much hunting found the skull, which he carefully replaced on the spot where he had discovered it. He was quite sure in his own mind that if the skull had dropped into the sea he would have been doomed. "All those arms that waved out there so desperately would have dragged me back into the water," he shudderingly remarked.[1]

When there are shipwrecks in the bay of Douarnenez it is believed by the fisherfolk that the sea carries the bodies of those who have been lost into the "Grotte-de-l'Autel," near Morgat, where their souls repose for eight days before departing for the next world. Woe be to him who disturbs their time of waiting by venturing into the cave during this period.

When a child was born at night, and if there was a moon, it was the custom in many places on the coast of Brittany for the oldest of the women present to place herself at the door, in order to observe the state of the sky at the exact moment when the new-born child made its appearance. If clouds covered the face of the moon at that minute there was no doubt that the poor infant would sooner or later end his days either by drowning or by being hanged![2]

An almost universal belief is that when a sailor dies at sea, gulls and curlews fly round his house and beat their wings against the windows. On the Ile-de-Sein they tell of the sound of the *Crierien*, i.e. the bones of sailors whose spirits are heard asking for burial. In some places it is believed that a storm cannot cease until the corpses of sailors who have died in a state of sin have been thrown up on some shore.

The bodies of those who have been drowned at sea or given burial in unconsecrated ground are doomed to wander eternally along the coast, and at night time one hears their piteous wailing. "Iou! Iou!" they cry. And when the sound is heard above the wind, the fisherfolk of Finistère say to themselves: "*E-man Iannic-*

---

[1] Anatole Le Braz, op. cit., vol. i, p. 398.   [2] Ibid., p. 391.

Cape Stiff, Ile-d'Ouessant

ann-od o iouall!" (There is *Iannic-ann-od* howling!) for that is the generic name they give to these wandering souls of drowned sailors.   They will do you no harm so long as you do not try to imitate their cries. If you do so more than twice they will break your neck!   On the Isle of Ouessant they say that "Iannic-ann-od" asks for some fire to warm himself with when he whispers beneath the door or whistles through the chinks of the window.

One might continue *ad infinitum* to give examples of the strange beliefs of the Breton sailors concerning the departed.   You will find them in the two volumes of Anatole Le Braz, *La Légende de la Mort chez les Bretons Armoricains,* from which I have here ventured to quote several examples of typical stories.   In conclusion I will describe the ceremony of *la proella,* which still takes place on the Ile-d'Ouessant.   As most of the male inhabitants are seamen in the mercantile marine a very large proportion die away from their island home.   As soon as news of a seaman's death has been officially received by the "Syndic des gens de mer," his oldest male relative is informed.   It is his duty to go round to all the houses on the island where relations of the deceased man live to announce the sad news to them, which is generally done with the following formula: "You are informed that this evening there will be the ceremony of the *proella*."

Not until after dark does he venture to approach the house of the widow.   He does so as if by stealth, knocking three times very gently on the window.   At length he enters the door and solemnly announces his tragic news: "To-night, my poor child, the *proella* will take place in your house."   The women of the neighbourhood who have been standing behind him now flock in, mingling their groans and cries with the mourning of the family.   This is called *mener le deuil.*   While it is going on the room is cleared out, a white cloth laid on the table, upon which are placed two napkins folded in the shape of a cross, in the centre of which is put a wax cross made of bits of the candles blessed and distributed on the feast of the Purification of Our Lady, 2nd February.   This cross is supposed to represent the dead man.   A plate, filled with holy water, with a bunch of leaves, is placed close by, and this, with two lighted candles, completes the funeral arrangements. From all corners of the island people begin to arrive. A sort of professional mourner, called a *prieuse*, recites all the usual prayers of the departed, often preaching a funeral oration, or *prézec*. The following morning the clergy and choir arrive as if for an ordinary funeral, to take away the "corpse," i.e. the little wax cross. The crowd of mourners follow, the men bareheaded, the women with their black shawls drawn close over their faces. A catafalque is erected in the midst of the church to receive the cross of the *proella*. Requiem Mass having been celebrated, the priest places the wax cross in a sort of urn-shaped box or casket that is fixed to the wall at the side of the chancel. Here it remains, either to the following All Souls' Day, or to some other solemn occasion such as a parochial mission or retreat, when the crosses in the casket are removed after vespers and solemnly transported to a special tomb in the middle of the cemetery, which serves as a common grave for these "symbols" of the bodies of the men of Ouessant who have died at sea far away from their island home in the midst of the Atlantic. A ceremony of a similar character takes place on the Ile-de-Sein, when one of the male inhabitants dies away from the island.

CHAPTER IV

BRETON SEAMEN IN THE FRENCH NAVY

In order to understand the life of maritime Brittany, it is essential
to have some idea of the organization and working of the *marine
de guerre*. There is scarcely a family anywhere along the coast
from Saint-Malo to Saint-Nazaire who has not at least one of its
sons serving in the navy, either as an *inscrit maritime*, an *engagé
volontaire*, or doing his *service*. Mothers will want to talk to you about
their boys, wives about their husbands. When you are travelling
you will be sure to meet one or more cheery *col bleus* going home
to their native village *en perm*, laden with parcels and the traditional
seaman's canvas kit-bag thrown over his shoulder. If you happen
to know something about their life, their surroundings, their
methods of promotion and pay, it is so much easier to enter into
conversation with them. Railway journeys on those bone-shaking
little *chemins de fer départementaux*, that would have been monotonous
and never-ending, will seem all too short, for Jean, Pierre, Yves, and
Louis will all have something to tell you, if you can overcome their
habitual Breton shyness by starting the conversation with a few
appropriate remarks and questions. A bottle of wine will be
produced from somewhere, and a loaf of bread, cold meat, and
sausage; you will be asked to share them. In return you will
offer your cigarettes, and before long you will be conversing and
exchanging ideas as if you were old friends. It is more than probable that these cheery sailors will be rather drunk: they will sing
songs and tell stories that are not always for the ears of *les jeunes
filles*, stories of their escapades ashore that would have delighted
Rabelais or provided Balzac with many a *conte drolatique*, stories
which, if blatantly coarse, at least have the tang of the sea about
them, and a freshness of youth that indicates little more than an
abundant source of animal spirits that is not necessarily vicious.

And when at last either you or your friends have reached your destination, there will be much handshaking and wishing of "Bon voyage."

"Au r'voir, m'sieur," they will cry, "au r'voir." . . . And as the train puffs and steams out of the station, if you wish to air your Breton, shout after them: "Au revoir, messieurs, kenavo."

Now there are three different ways in which your travelling companions may have joined the lower-deck ranks of the French *marine de guerre*. They may be classified as:

(1) Naval conscription (*inscription maritime*).
(2) Voluntary recruiting (*engagements volontaires*).
(3) Annual contingent furnished by compulsory service.

The majority of boys who live on the coast, and whose fathers are seafarers, are enrolled on what is known as *la matricule* as soon as they are ten years old. They are then classed as *inscrits provisoires*, with the rating of *mousse* until they are seventeen, *novice* during their eighteenth year. After a period of not less than eighteen months afloat, either fishing or in the mercantile marine, the *inscrit provisoire* is promoted to be an *inscrit définitif*.

For the sake of example, let us imagine a boy whom we will call Yves Ménou, hailing from the Ile-de-Sein, where practically all the men are seafarers. As soon as he leaves school he will go to sea in his father's boat, as *mousse*, working with him until he reaches the age of twenty, when he will be called up to do his military service. As he is already enrolled on *la matricule* of the *inscription maritime*, he will be drafted at once to the depot at Brest, to which base he belongs, and will be given the rating of *matelot de 3me classe*.

The organization of the *inscription maritime* was introduced by Colbert about 1650, and is now controlled from four *régions maritimes*:

(1) Dunkerque, Le Havre, Cherbourg;
(2) Saint-Servan, Nantes, Lorient;
(3) Marseilles, Toulon, Corsica;
(4) Algeria.

Each *région* is subdivided into *arrondissements* and *quartiers*.

Yves Ménou's time of compulsory service in the navy will consist of seven years in all, i.e. five years of active service (*période obligatoire*) and two years on the Reserve (*période de disponibilité*). The first period will not be altogether continuous, and the second period he will only be called occasionally for a few weeks. After this he will pass definitely into the Reserve, only to be called up in case of mobilization.

There are many advantages for a fisherman to be an *inscrit maritime*. He has the right to sell fish without paying certain taxes, to reserve certain parts of the foreshore for breeding oysters or other purposes in connection with his craft, he can capture sea-birds. These privileges also apply to the widows and unmarried orphans of *inscrits maritimes*. After twenty-five years at sea, and having reached the age of fifty, he can draw a pension known as a *demi-solde*. He is also insured in case of accident and illness. If his family numbers more than five children under the age of eleven, he receives extra.

But Yves has a brother whom we will call Pierre. He does not feel any wish to follow his father's calling as a fisherman, but the sea is in his blood, and so it is decided that he shall join the *marine de guerre* as an *engagé volontaire*. He is fourteen and a half years old, and his parents agree that they will send him to the *école des mousses* at Brest, where he will receive a general education in addition to a specialized training. Voluntary engagements are for a period of three to six years, five years being the normal period. But boys who join the *école des mousses* sign on for ten years and are classed as *apprentis-marins* until they leave this school, after which they become *apprentis-marins* or *apprentis-mécaniciens*, according to which branch of the service they decide to follow. After three years at the *école des mousses*, and if he has not been sent back to his family as being unfitted for life in the navy, a rather serious matter for the parents, as they are bound to refund the cost of their son's training, the boy will be obliged to sign on for a period of ten years' service.

Another brother, Jean in this same family, shows an interest in machinery. Neither does he want to become a fisherman, so at the age of fifteen he is sent off to the *école des mécaniciens* on very much the same terms as his brother Pierre in the *école des mousses*. He does well in his examinations, and soon passes from the ranks of *matelots de 1re classe* to that of *quartier-maître*.

Both these boys had to apply to what corresponds to our "Commodore of the Barracks" (the *Commandant du dépôt des équipages de la Flotte*) at Brest, the area to which they belong in the *inscription maritime*, before they could enter. Having received a favourable answer they went off to Brest for examination and the carrying out of the necessary formalities, more complicated in France than with us. During this period they were lodged at the expense of the navy in barracks.

There is yet another brother, Louis, who wants to become an electrician, his uncle having a shop. He will do his period of compulsory service in the *marine de guerre* for exactly the same time and under the same conditions as if he had gone to the army. He will be admitted as an *apprenti-marin*, but having a definite trade he will get a *spécialité*. He is a sharp, intelligent lad. After a year's service he will get his *bréveté provisoire*, and when he goes home *en permission* he will proudly show a red stripe on the top of his left sleeve. Next time he comes back on leave you will notice he has two red stripes, one on each arm. He is now a *matelot de 1re classe*, having obtained his *breveté élémentaire*.

Here is a rough idea of the system of promotion in the lower-deck ratings of the French navy with the approximate ratings in the British navy:

Apprenti-marin	= Boy Seaman
Matelot de 3me classe	= Ordinary Seaman
Matelot de 2me classe	= Able Seaman
Matelot de 1re classe	= Leading Seaman
Quartier-maître	= 2nd Class Petty Officer
Second maître	= 1st Class Petty Officer
Maître	= Warrant Officer
Premier maître	= Petty Officer
Maître principal	= Mate

Every six months there is an examination, familiarly referred to as the *passage à la chambre*. Those who get through the ordeal most satisfactorily are given the *mention apte*, and are promoted to the next highest rating or *grade*. These promotions, together with the *brevet* for *specialités*, mean an increase of pay. Certain cases have been known where a lad passed rapidly through all the stages from an *apprenti-marin* to that of *quartier-maître* before his sixteenth year. But these are exceptional.

The system of pay in the French navy is a rather complicated one, at least for an outsider to easily grasp the details of its working.

Each man on joining receives a book known as his *livret de solde*, in which is entered up the debit and credit against his name, the *délégation*, or quarterly payment to his family being also deducted from this.

He also receives his *numéro matricule*, briefly referred to as *le matricule*. If he is an *inscrit maritime*, i.e. definitely registered at one of the ports on the coast, his *matricule* will read as follows: "41, 259—P," which means he belongs to Paimpol. On the other hand, a *col-bleu* who is not an *inscrit maritime*, but merely doing his period of compulsory service in the navy, will have the number of his depot on his *matricule* instead of the initial of his port, e.g. 106598—2 indicates that he belongs to the depot at Brest.

Life on board a modern French battleship, cruiser, or destroyer is not so very different from that in a similar type of ship in the British navy. Details of routine vary slightly; possibly the work is harder and more continuous. The British bluejacket would certainly grouse at the way the French *col-bleu* is fed, whereas I do not know how Jean, François, Yves, and Louis would care for the meals provided for Bill, Jim, Ted, and Harry!

Every morning at 5.30, when most of the folk ashore are still in bed, the strident shouting of the *maître*, "Branlebas debout, debout," rouses the sleeping men out of their warm *bois de lits* (hammocks), accompanied by the sound of the *binious* (bugles). All hands turn out, blankets are rolled up, hammocks lashed up, and stowed away with amazing rapidity. If they are late the *second maître* will have noted their *numéro*.

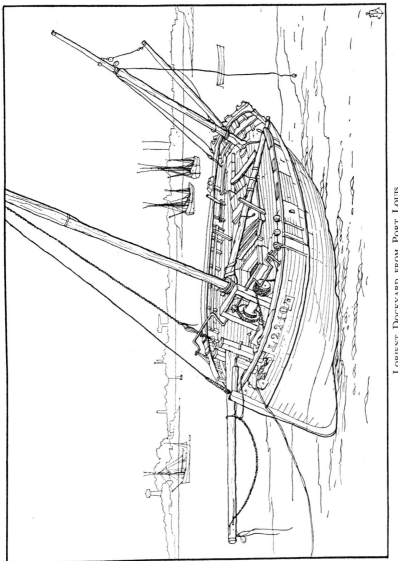

LORIENT DOCKYARD FROM PORT LOUIS

From the stuffy atmosphere of the *postes d'équipage* the "*gâs*" hurry along the deck towards the cook's galley, where the fragrant smell of *jus* (hot coffee) greets their nostrils. The *officier de service* has already drunk a cup to see if the beverage is fit for human consumption; if he is satisfied with its quality, then it is good enough for every one!

Groups of *col - bleus* in trousers and striped *tricots* stand around the galley doorway, sniffing the coffee, laughing and joking: "T'as vu ça, hein? C'est pas un jus d'oignons qu'on aura ce matin, je t'en réponds," and other similar sparks of Gallic wit that will not bear translating here.

Standing over his stove, the cook plunges his huge ladle into the deep cauldron-like "kettle" in which the coffee is simmering, distributing the brown liquid to the men who are waiting with their metal *gamelles*.

They push and shove each other: one man wants more than his share. "Combien à ta plat?" exclaims the cook. "Cinq? Une louchée quand même."

Ratings of all types are grouped around drinking the steaming hot coffee, in which they soak their hunks of dry bread, for such is the meagre breakfast of a French bluejacket, upon which he has to satisfy any pangs of hunger until his dinner at midday. Some of the men stand, others squat on the deck, the rest seat themselves on coils of rope or anything else handy.

Meanwhile boats are being got ready; *permissionnaires* (liberty men) have to come off; a picket boat is already alongside with steam up; stores must be fetched from the *arsenal*, mails from the post office *en ville*.

A whistle blows, *bidons* and *gamelles* are stowed away and shoved back in their racks: a hasty toilet (*briquage de gueule* as it is familiarly termed) is gone through in the modern and up-to-date wash-houses with their rows of basins and taps: for no longer do we find the primitive ablutions performed over a bucket of water as in bygone days. A short interval for a smoke, and then at 6.30 *les binious* blow, nasal orders are repeated through loud - speakers: "Aux postes de lavage tout le monde." . . . "Bas les souliers." . . .

With trousers turned up to the knee, armed with long-handed scrubbers, hundreds of barefooted men are soon engaged on the chilly work of scrubbing decks; hoses are playing, water flows everywhere, while others are occupied in polishing brasswork and such-like jobs. At eight o'clock the bugle sounds attention, *au drapeau*, and every one stands bareheaded while *les couleurs* are slowly hoisted, the band striking up *Au Drapeau*.

Once again the loud-speakers raise their voices, "Aux exercices," and the various parties of men are "piped" to the forenoon's work; some for painting ship, others to clean flats, others for gunnery or torpedo practice, and so on; everything being arranged on the daily *cahier de service* by the officer in charge of the *service intérieur*. Work goes on until 10.45, when the bugles sound to stop work. Dinner is then served, a substantial and generally well-cooked meal of two courses, soup, meat, and vegetables, with a quarter-bottle of *pinard* (red wine) for each man, after which *bidons* and *gamelles* are cleared away, pipes and cigarettes produced, until one o'clock, when *les binious* again summon the ship's company to their afternoon work. About 1.30 p.m. takes place the sometimes disagreeable business of the *règlements de compte* for those who have been unlucky enough to have their names *sur le cahier* for some breach of ship's discipline —"commander's defaulters," as it is termed in the British navy. Supper, a meal similar in quantity and quality to dinner, is served at five. Every other day the *permissionnaires* (liberty men) go ashore at 4.45, while those left on board amuse themselves as they choose —read, smoke, write letters, play cards—until the hammocks are slung (*dégagé du branlebas*) at 7 p.m. The day's work is over once more, and within an hour or so, Jean, Louis, Yves, and François are rolled up in their blankets fast asleep.

The French naval officer of to-day is perhaps more comfortably housed than his British brother, at least such is my own impression as an outsider. There is always a certain indefinable "something" that differentiates the *carré* of a modern French warship from even the most up-to-date wardroom in one of our own ships: a certain quality—how can one describe it? (a *cachet* one would say in French; we have no English word that exactly conveys the idea)—which may be nothing more than the material expression of racial temperament and feeling.

But, on the other hand, the standard of comfort that now exists for the lower-deck rating in the British navy is certainly lacking in the French *marine de guerre*.   And perhaps the men are all the better for it?

CHAPTER V

MANY authors have described the life on board the old Iceland schooners and "terre-neuvas," but few have managed to convey the atmosphere with the vividness and realism of Pierre Loti.   In the opening chapter of *Pêcheur d'Islande* he thrusts the reader without any sort of preliminary introduction right into the midst of a group of five burly fishermen who are sitting around the table in the dark, smelly cabin of the "goëlette" *Marie* off the coast of Iceland.   It is night time and dark outside.   The old vessel is gently rolling on the long Atlantic swell.   A hanging lamp, the only source of illumination, is swaying to and fro.   A fire is burning in a stove; the steam from the wet clothes of the five men mingling with the smoke from their short black clay pipes.   Their massive table takes up almost all the space in the cabin.   There is just room on either side to sit down on the wooden lockers fixed to the oak partitions behind which lay the dark bunks, which have the appearance of niches in a funeral vault, waiting for a coffin to be put in.   All the woodwork is rough and worn, impregnated with damp and salt, shiny and polished with the constant rubbing of hands.

They have been drinking.   Their bowls are filled with wine or cider.   Their faces are lit up with a comfortable glow.   Leaning over the table they are discussing in Breton various matters concerning women in general and the physical pleasures of married life in particular.   Against one of the timbers hung a china image of the Blessed Virgin and Child, occupying as it were the place of honour on a bracket.   She is dressed in a bright robe of red and blue, the only patch of colour in this dark mass of sombre grey. Nailed to the bracket are shabby bouquets of artificial flowers and a rosary.

67

All the five men are wearing thick blue woollen jerseys tucked into their trousers. On their heads are sou'westers. On the wooden deck above them is the pattering sound of rain. All around, nothing but an infinite desolation of black night and dark water. A copper clock fastened to a bulkhead points to 11 p.m.

It is the feast of·the Assumption of Our Lady, 15th August, and

TERRE-NEUVA "ROUZIC" AT SAINT-SERVAN

they have had a rest from their accustomed work of fishing. To-morrow the hard toil will begin all over again. The *patron* calls the *mousse* to refill the pipes with tobacco, and pours out more wine into the bowls on the table. . . .

And throughout the rest of the book the life on board this "goëlette," fishing for cod in the far northern waters off Iceland, is described to us with a vividness that never palls, no matter how often one re-reads this famous novel of the sea. It is probably known to most of my readers, but if they have not read it they should do so, for nowhere else does one gain such a true picture of the life of the Breton cod fishermen as it was fifty or sixty years ago, before the coming of steam and motor.

. . . .

(1) *Newfoundland Banks Fisheries.* Until a few years ago the cod fisheries were carried on in various parts of the Atlantic in the neighbourhood of Newfoundland: off the Bonnet Flamand, the Grand Banc, Banc-a-Vert, Banc-de-Saint-Pierre, Cape Breton, the mouth of the River Saint Lawrence, and around the Magdalen Islands, but recently the tendency has been for the sphere of operations to be confined much more to the area of the Platier Bank, 52 deg. W. by 44 deg. N.

The vessels taking part in this fishing are divided into two classes: those coming over from France, those owned and stationed at Saint-Pierre-Miquelon. The latter are generally manned with Breton crews.

In the first division are to be found:

(a) Sailing craft: "trois-mâts" (barquentines), from Saint-Malo, Saint-Servan, Cancale (to mention only the ports in Brittany).

(b) Steam-trawlers: "chalutiers."

In addition to the French fishing vessels the Newfoundland Banks are frequented by the Canadian, Portuguese, and American schooners.

The older type of sailing vessels, all of them barquentines, known as "terre-neuvas," provided little or no comfort or convenience for the men who lived on board them during seven or eight months every year. All they aimed at was to accommodate as many men as possible in the smallest possible space, and to keep out the cold. The result was the crew were always overcrowded in a manner impossible to believe, unless one has actually seen some of these older class of vessels. Two men had to share the same berth in these stuffy, dog-kennel-like quarters. There was practically no provision for either light or ventilation.

In the year 1907 the Government passed a law which laid down certain minimum conditions that must be complied with, both regarding the conditions on board and the rations provided. As far as possible, light and ventilation were insisted upon, and a separate berth for each man. The owners did their best to carry out these regulations on board their ships. But the law could not change the character and habits of the men. Accustomed from boyhood to living in conditions often little better than those prevailing in pigsties, the *Terre-Neuvas* resented this well-meaning attempt for their welfare. What was good enough for their grandfathers was good enough for them. Fresh air was dangerous. One had plenty of it on deck. So they took care to close up all skylights and other means of ventilation so as to make themselves snug and cosy down below.

Before long things were as bad as ever. Gradually, however, the men began to realize that the Government had no sinister intentions in demanding the carrying-out of these regulations. Very slowly an improvement began to take place on board, especially when prizes were offered for the *bonne tenue* of the ships. They began to see that it might be to their own advantage to keep their vessels cleaner. One of the strongest motives that made them resist any change was the deeply-rooted conviction that a clean ship was unlucky, and that the cod were attracted by the smell of rotten and decayed fish lying about on the decks! Nowadays, all supplies put on board a "terre-neuvas" leaving France are subject to a strict examination both regarding quantity and quality. Certain restrictions are laid down as to the amount of alcohol carried, the consumption of which had reached an alarming amount.

The system of payment on these *terre-neuvas* is rather a complicated one, based on a co-operative plan, details of which are not everywhere the same. The general idea is that each individual member of the crew receives a definite sum, calculated according to the success of the season's fishing. Since 1910 Saint-Malo, Saint-Servan, and Paimpol have adopted a 25 per cent basis of payment. At Cancale a different system prevails. It would take too long to go into all the details of this. As a rule each man receives a certain share of the profits in relation to the actual number of fish he has caught. Thus each member of the crew is encouraged by the hope of individual gain. It is a less "fraternal" system than the one that prevails at Fécamp in Normandy, where each man is paid 5 per cent of the total profits of the season's catch, quite independent of what he may have taken himself. The abuses that used to take place in the olden days when large sums of money were advanced to the crews before sailing, and which were generally squandered, have been practically abolished. At the present time only a minimum sum is advanced to each member of the crew in proportion to his rank.

Before the war there were as many as three hundred French sailing vessels engaged in the Newfoundland fisheries. Since 1918 the number of steam trawlers has greatly increased, and before long the older "voiliers" may have become a memory of the past. At the time of writing there are no more than seventy-three of them left at Saint-Malo and Saint-Servan, sixty-three being engaged in the Newfoundland fisheries.

Their departure takes place every year about the second week in March. Their passage across the Atlantic takes about four weeks, given good weather. Fishing off the Banks starts in April. The first thing to be done is to lay in a supply of bait; a small shell-fish, known as *bulot*, being generally used for this purpose. It is obtained at Sydney, Nova Scotia, or in the Magdalen Islands. The American and Newfoundland fishermen, however, make use of salt herring, or another kind of shell-fish found on the sandy bottoms of the Platier Bank, south-east of the Grand Banc. Experience and luck are the only way of determining the fishing-grounds; but the cod is a voracious fish once located.

Off the Banks of Newfoundland, the actual fishing is always carried on from small boats known as "doris." They leave their parent ships every morning at dawn. Each vessel carries twelve "doris." At sea they are stowed away on deck, one inside the other. They are a long, almost flat-bottomed boat, and capable of standing almost any sea when properly handled. Every "doris" is obliged to carry a compass, a supply of biscuits and water, and one spare oar. Two men form their crew, the *patron* and the *avant*, the latter usually no more than a young boy, but who must not be less than sixteen years of age.

Fogs spring up without any warning off the Banks, and a "doris" may easily be lost for hours, or even days, if she goes too far away from the "voilier." Hence the need of carrying supplies on board.

"Doris" of the Terre-Neuva "Gloire à Dieu" at Saint-Servan

Having rowed away a certain distance, the lines, baited the night before, are shot. They hang more or less perpendicularly from a buoy, not unlike the spokes of a wheel. The "doris" then returns to the "voilier," and for the rest of the day the men are hard at work salting and cleaning the cod caught the previous day, and baiting the lines for to-morrow's fishing. The crew have scarcely a moment's rest. Towards evening they embark again in their tiny boats, haul in their lines, and bring back the fish, which is piled up on the deck. Supper is then served, and the men are able to take a short night's rest before starting work again next morning. Most of them are so worn out that they do not bother to remove even their oilskins, and just throw themselves down in their bunks fully dressed. Their only chance of a respite from work is during bad weather, when it is too rough to fish. During the summer months, fog and rain are very frequent off the Banks, for there may be days when the sun is not visible and a damp, clammy mist hangs over the sea. Yet, despite the hardships of the life, the men are healthy as a rule, diseases being rare, but wounds and accidents frequent. Each vessel carries a medicine chest, but few captains have any medical knowledge or experience. In cases of serious accidents, a captain will try to get back to Saint-Pierre-Miquelon. But often he is too late.

In the year 1894 was founded the *Société des Œuvres de Mer*, with the special object of attending to the material, moral, and religious welfare of the fishermen off the Newfoundland Banks. Ever since then, one or more hospital ships have been commissioned every season, and they spend the summer cruising about among the fishing fleets. A fishermen's institute, or *Maison du Marin*, is maintained at Saint-Pierre-Miquelon. Since the war the Œuvres de Mer have only been able to retain one hospital ship in commission—the *Sainte-Jeanne-d'Arc*. She carries a doctor and chaplain, and acts as postman to the French fishing vessels by distributing their mail.

(2) *Iceland and Greenland Fisheries*. The Iceland fisheries are carried on between the longitude 14 W., 45 W., and latitude 5. The chief difference between the Iceland fishing and that off Newfoundland is that, owing to the great depth of the ocean, vessels cannot anchor and are always under sail or steam. The season starts in February.

During the month of March the fishing is carried on off the Westmann Islands, to the extreme south of Iceland. The fleets then move westwards as far as Faxafjord. During the months of May and June they are fishing more to the eastward round about Hwalsbak, a little below the latitude of Faskrudsfjord, some going

as far as Seidisfjord. Other vessels prefer the west coast of the
island in the neighbourhood of Patrixfjord and Isafjord. When
July arrives they all gather in the Bay of Reykjavik, remaining
there until the end of August. At the close of this month the
majority of them return to France, a few continuing to fish on the
same grounds as where they started in February.

The type of vessel fitted out from Paimpol for the Iceland fishing
is smaller than that employed off Newfoundland. The sailing
craft are generally "goëlettes" (schooners),[1] or "dundees" (ketches).[2]
But every year their number grows less, partly owing to the competition of the steam trawlers from Dunkerque and Gravelines.
Before the war, about twenty to thirty sailing vessels were fitted
out from Paimpol and Binic. To-day they number no more than
eleven. Despite their small size, the "dundees" used always to
be the favourite type of craft with the Iceland fishermen. They
were easier to handle than the schooner-rigged "goëlettes," and
better at sea in rough weather. But the conditions on board were
terribly crowded, and only one life-boat was carried, quite insuffi-
cient to accommodate the crew in case of accident. In the more
recent type of vessel conditions have been improved, as in the
"terre-neuvas."

Steam trawlers first made their appearance off the coast of
Iceland in 1903. They were small vessels with crews of twenty
men. The modern steam trawlers now engaged in the Iceland and
Greenland fisheries are magnificent vessels, superior both as regards
size and equipment to those belonging to any other nation. A fine
example of one of these trawlers is the *Téméraire*, page 75 (965
tons, with a crew of 50 men).

At Paimpol, which has always been the chief port for the Iceland
fisheries, the crews are paid on the following system: One-third of
the total profit of the season's catch is reserved for the crew, each
man receiving a sum calculated according to the number of cod
he has caught himself. The other two-thirds go to the owner of
the vessel, who has to pay for the upkeep and the cost of material,
etc. As a general rule the system seems to work satisfactorily.

[1] See page 12.   [2] See page 124.

STEAM TRAWLER "TÉMÉRAIRE"

Despite this, however, the Iceland fishing at Paimpol is going down every year and fewer vessels are being fitted out.[1] The only reason for this would appear to be the competition of the steam trawlers from other ports, and the unwillingness, or inability from want of capital, of the Paimpolais to change their method of fishing.

One of the chief dangers that confront the Iceland fisherman is the constant and sudden changes in the weather in these far northern waters. With scarcely any warning the wind shifts, and a dead calm gives way to a wind of hurricane force. Blinding snowstorms are also frequent.

As we have explained already, the actual fishing has to be carried on from the ship, and not by means of "doris" as in the "terre-neuvas." Strong lines with two hooks are used, with any sort of bait that may be found, fish or sea-birds. The cod is not fastidious! The Icelanders themselves generally prefer to bait their lines with salt herring. Like every other fisherman, those of Iceland are intensely conservative, and nothing will induce them to forsake their usual fishing-grounds, even if they have no luck and the presence of cod elsewhere should be reported by wireless. Year after year the same programme, the same course, is regularly followed from the beginning of the season to the end. While the lines are shot, the vessel sails on the same tack in order to give the men more freedom of action.

On the steam trawlers there is not much difference in the actual life and routine to what we have already described in the sailing craft, except that owing to the enormous quantity of fish that is caught at once, and the consequent crowded state of the decks, it is often necessary for the vessel to steam back to port or to some sheltered anchorage before the men can start cleaning and salting the catch. During the season, *chasseurs* (carriers) take on board the salted cod from the trawlers and carry it back to France.

In many ways the Iceland fishing, both on the "goëlettes" and on the "chalutiers," is far less laborious than that of Newfoundland, the chief reason being that no "doris" are used. Neither is it so monotonous. Fogs are less frequent and the weather, although

[1] See end of chapter for number of vessels now engaged in Iceland fisheries.

stormy and squally, has fine intervals. Again, both steam trawlers and "dundees" make frequent trips to port. The crews have spells ashore at Reykjavik or Faskrudfjord. There are fewer accidents and less sickness among the men. Medical assistance is provided for the French fishermen, by the *Société des Hôpitaux Français d'Islande*, which maintains hospitals at Reykjavik, Faskrudsfjord, and on the Wastmann Isles. Before the war the Société des Œuvres de Mer sent a hospital ship to Iceland every summer and provided a hospital at Faskrudsfjord. But both these have now been given up. Until 1929 the fishery protection cruiser *Ville d'Ys* used to spend part of her time cruising off Iceland and the rest of the year off the Newfoundland banks, in order to settle any disputes or difficulties that might occur among the fishing vessels. But the present arrangement is that Iceland, Newfoundland, and the North Sea each have their own fishery protection cruiser.

COD FISHERIES FROM BRETON PORTS

Statistics for 1930

	No.	Men
A. STEAM TRAWLERS.		
Saint-Malo—Saint-Servan—Cancale	6	302
B. SAILING VESSELS.		
(1) *Iceland:* Paimpol	7	176
(2) *Greenland:*		
Paimpol	4	100
Saint-Malo—Saint-Servan—Cancale	10	346
(3) *Newfoundland:* Saint-Malo—Saint-Servan—Cancale . .	63	2010
Total	90	2934
Total number of vessels fitted out in France for cod fisheries in 1930	141	4998

CHAPTER VI

THE BRETON SARDINE FISHERIES

THE sardine fisheries of Brittany date from remote antiquity. The sardine has been valued as an article of food for many centuries, although the present-day method of preserving it in oil was only introduced less than a hundred years ago.

The honour of having discovered that, as well as meat and vegetables, fish might be preserved by hermetically sealing it up in tins, is due to a certain Monsieur Blanchard of Lorient, who made the first experiments about 1825. Previously sardines were either dried and pressed in casks, or smoked and cured like herrings in "sauce" and kept in barrels. The first sardine factory was opened at Les Sables-d'Olonne in 1832, to be followed later by Belle-Ile-en-Mer (1834), La Turballe (1841), and Concarneau (1840).

Until 1870 there were not more than thirty sardine factories on the coast of Brittany, but between 1888 and 1901 the industry increased with amazing rapidity, the number of boats being more than trebled during these thirteen years. Every Breton seemed to think that he was going to make his fortune out of the sardine. Peasants flocked into the ports from the surrounding country-side, more and more factories were built, when suddenly the crash came. There was a slump in sardines: no fish, no work, and no money. After some time the industry recovered its former prosperity, and is still as great a source of profit to the country as ever before.

A certain German writer, in the *Mitteilungen des Deutschen See-fischerei-Vereins*, once described the sardine as the "most international of fish." He was right. The sardine swims all over the world—in oil, not in water! There is now no more popular and universal article of preserved food than this little silver fish. Probably more than seventy thousand persons are engaged in the sardine industry, including over forty thousand fishermen.

78

SARDINE BOATS AT AUDIERNE

Very little is actually known about the life and habits of the sardine, despite the enormous number caught annually. They are to be found all the year round off the coasts of Spain, Portugal, and Morocco, and for more than three-quarters of the year they can be caught in the Bay of Biscay. The popular and generally accepted theory, although disputed by scientists, is that the sardine migrates northward from May onwards. In August and September it is to be found in vast shoals off the coast of Finistère. It is quite certain that they come there, but just how has never been conclusively settled, any more than the presence of herring in the North Sea in the early autumn.

The sardines caught in the Bay of Biscay during the late summer are only half grown and have not yet spawned. They are generally known as *sardines de rogue*, since they are caught with bait called *rogue*. Those caught in the autumn are referred to as *sardines de dérive*, as they are fatter and captured with a larger-meshed drift net. It is difficult to convey any idea of the number of sardines that are to be found in a shoal, or its density. The little sardine is always pursued by enemies: sea-birds, dolphins (known as *béluga* in Brittany), and the red tunny. Far more are destroyed by natural enemies than by the fisherman. A shoal of sardines may be as long as three kilometres, and the same breadth. Wherever there is a shoal of sardine there will always be found *bélugas*.

As we have repeated so often in these pages, there is no more conservative seaman anywhere else in the world than the mariner of Brittany, and the sardine fisherman is no exception to the rest of his brethren. The same methods of capture are employed to-day as were in use centuries ago, except for a few modifications in the type of boat employed and the introduction of motor power.

About the year 1877 cod's roe, commonly known as *rogue* or *rave*, was introduced as bait. The sardine net is of gossamer-like texture, fine as gauze, light and delicate as the little silver fish it captures. In order to deceive the sardine it is "tanned" ("barked," one would say in Scotland) a bright blue colour, so as not to be so conspicuous in the vividly clear water that is so frequent off the coast of Brittany in the summer months. The nets average about 25 fathoms in length and 450 meshes deep.   Each boat carries about fifteen nets of all sizes of mesh, varying from 32 to 72 millimetres.

The picturesque costume of the sardine fishermen has been immortalized in thousands of paintings.   Artists seem quite unable to resist the amazing colour-scheme to be found in all the ports of Finistère and Morbihan.   The trousers and jumpers of the men

OLD TYPE OF DOUARNENEZ SARDINE BOATS

vary in hue from the brightest orange vermilion to the palest rose pink, and are decorated with every imaginable sort of patch!   At Douarnenez, until recently, blue jumpers and trousers were worn, but within recent years, red seems to have become more and more common everywhere.   Grey or black woollen jerseys, and black or blue bérets complete the costume,[1] together with clumsy wooden sabots.

At sea oilskin trousers, known as *cotillons*, are put on, also a

[1] Nowadays usually replaced by the ordinary sailor's peaked cap or the Basque béret.

primitive sort of sea-boot, made out of wooden sabots, with oilskin uppers, picturesque, but, one would imagine, extremely awkward and cumbersome. Here, again, the younger men have adopted the more comfortable rubber sea-boot. An oilskin coat, with a hood attached, is worn in rough weather and serves also for warmth.

The greatest difficulty the sardine fishermen have to put up with is the constant presence of the *bélugas*, always on the watch and ever ready to destroy their nets. The red tunny is almost as tiresome an enemy. It leaps into the air and jumps through the nets, tearing them to pieces. Nothing seems to frighten them, and they will follow a boat for a whole day. Since 1875 the Breton fishermen have made use of various artificial baits in the sardine fishing, the most popular of these being *farine d'arachide*, a fine powder made from peanuts. When thrown overboard on either side of the boat the water turns into a milky fluid. The *béluga* is not able to make out the sardine so easily, and this prevents the wholesale destruction of nets. For many years controversy was waged regarding these artificial baits, many curers maintaining that the fish swelled and were spoiled. The sardine is such a delicate fish that it has to be cured as fresh as possible and taken direct to the factories on being landed. Only a very small quantity is sold for immediate consumption, and what is not wanted for curing is thrown away and wasted.

Imagine that you are staying in any one of the sardine ports on the south coast of Brittany. You are roused from your sleep some time between two and five in the morning by the "clomp, clomp" of wooden sabots on the stone paving of the street beneath your window. If you are sufficiently curious you rise from your bed and peer out. In some of the houses dim lights are twinkling. In the darkness you make out groups of men walking in the direction of the harbour. Each man carries a small bundle; his food for the day's fishing, generally a hunk of bread. In addition to bread, fish soup (*cotriade*), is prepared on a small stove or a fire lighted on a flat stone. There is a barrel of water on each sardine boat. When at sea this is the ordinary drink, no matter how much wine, cider, rum, and brandy a man may consume when he is on shore.

On the larger "sardiniers" as many as twelve men are carried, i.e. two crews. On the smaller old-fashioned sail-boats only seven men make up a crew. They are paid on a share basis.

Having got away from the harbour the fleet makes for the fishing-grounds, arriving there by sunrise so as to be ready to start fishing as soon as it is light. On all the large motor "sardiniers" two *canots*, or fifteen-foot rowing-boats, are carried. Five men embark in each of these and start work: two men are at the oars, two men amidships shoot the nets, and one man in the stern throws out the *rogue* (bait) already referred to above. They continue rowing. The net, weighted with lead, hangs down like a vertical wall in the water astern of the boat. From time to time it will be hauled in to see if the fish are there. The sardines, like herring and mackerel, try to swim through the fine mesh of the net, attracted by the *rogue*, and are caught by their gills.

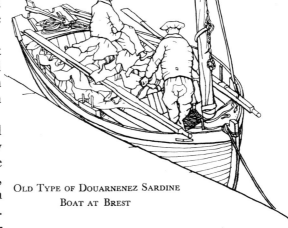

After a while the net is hauled on board and the sardines shaken out into the bottom of the boat.

Fishing goes on all the morning. Early in the afternoon the fleet sails back to port, generally arriving in harbour about 4 p.m.

OLD TYPE OF DOUARNENEZ SARDINE
BOAT AT BREST

In the old days fishing was always carried on from the "sardinier" itself. Masts were lowered and sweeps got out to keep the boat head to wind. The crew paid out the nets, while the skipper stood at the stern, scattering the *rogue* like a farmer sowing seed, never forgetting to make the sign of the cross before starting.

I am told that the blue nets, so loved by the artist, did not make their appearance much before the close of the last century. Previous to that they were tanned in the ordinary way. It is quite probable that the blue nets are less visible in the water than the brown ones, as larger fish, such as herring, sprats, and mackerel, are sometimes caught in the sardine nets during the daytime, whereas normally they can only be caught at night.

The nets are kept in the stern of the boat in a sort of wooden chest which can be lifted out. On the smaller sardine boats there is no cabin. If the crew do not return to their home port to land their catch, and are obliged to spend the night on board, they rig up a kind of tent by stretching a sail. The men sleep on the bottom boards. If it is cold they wrap themselves up in their long hooded capes made of sail-canvas and lined with green blanket.

Early in the afternoon crowds begin to assemble around the quays of every sardine port to watch for the return of the fleet. It is always a wonderfully picturesque sight, no matter whether they are beating in against the wind or scudding along with all sail set with an after breeze. As soon as a boat gets within the breakwater or harbour, the *canot* (or *annexe* as they are sometimes called) is cast off, the boat made fast to her moorings, the sails lowered and the nets hoisted up to the masts to dry, "blowing out in the breeze like cigarette smoke," as an English writer happily described them.[1]

The *canot*, laden with fish, is rowed ashore, moored to the quay, and the sardines taken up to the factory in baskets. Here they are headed and cleaned and sorted, the work being carried on by young girls whose ages vary from ten to fifteen. The fish are then soaked in brine, and arranged, tail upwards, in wire trays holding about fifty each, ranged on long hand-barrows in the sun if it is fine, in brick ovens if it is wet. The trays are next dipped into very hot oil, than drained off, and again dried in the sun or

[1] Leslie Richardson, *Brittany and the Loire*, p. 134.

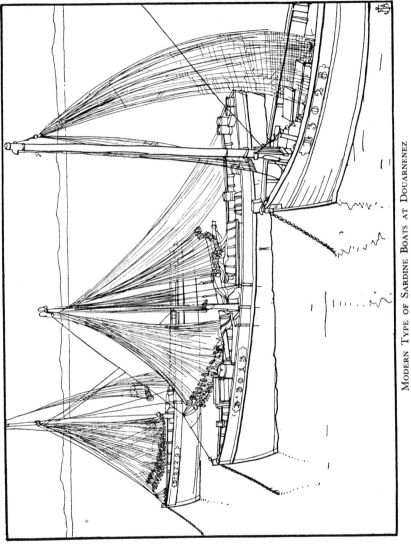

MODERN TYPE OF SARDINE BOATS AT DOUARNENEZ

by artificial heat. When thoroughly dry they are packed in the familiar tin boxes known all the world over, filled up with hot oil, and then hermetically sealed and packed for transport. The sizes are gauged by *le quart*, small ones at twelve, larger at sixteen. The quality of a box of sardines is not due to the fish inside it, but to the oil in which it is soaked. For the cheaper sort cotton oil is used, for the better brands the finest olive oil from the Italian or French Riviera.

The women employed in the factories often have to work all night when the fishing is good. They also repair and make nets. The infuriating keys sold with the tins of sardines mostly come from Nantes.

CHAPTER VII

THE BRETON TUNNY FISHERIES

THE Breton tunny fisheries are of quite recent introduction. Tunny fishing in the Bay of Biscay was started at La Rochelle and Sables-d'Olonne about forty years ago. Their success inspired the men of the Ile-de-Groix to follow their example, and later on Concarneau.

The fish caught in the Bay of Biscay, the white tunny (*Thynnus alalonga*) is different to the red tunny (*Thynnus orcynus*) captured in the Mediterranean. The flesh of the latter is darker in colour. Both fish, however, have red muscles like those of a mammal. There is no more full-blooded fish than the tunny. Its temperature is as high as that of many animals. Both kinds belong to the mackerel family (*Scombridæ*), pursuing their prey like the tuna of the Pacific, and are very fast swimmers. The Mediterranean tunny is usually caught near shore by means of stake-nets (*madragues*). The Atlantic tunny is captured on a hook and lives in deep water as far off as a hundred to a hundred and fifty miles from land. The average weight of the latter is about thirty pounds, the red tunny being much heavier. At one time the tunny was caught nearer land in the Bay of Biscay. The fishermen maintain that it now keeps far out owing to the presence of oil on the surface of the water. It seems that the fish generally swim in a north-easterly direction. But it is not a real or continuous migration, their movements being regulated by a search for food, usually shrimps. It is uncertain where the tunny come from previous to their arrival in the Bay of Biscay.

By the time the fishing commences they have already spawned. There is no more voracious fish than the tunny. He will swallow anything. Sometimes bits of tin and paper are found in his belly. He swims on the surface of the water, only diving below in cold weather or in rain.

The average size of a Breton tunny boat is from fifty to ninety tons. They are always increasing in size; but so far none of them have been fitted with motors, the men maintaining that the noise of the engine would frighten the fish. The older craft were schooner-rigged with three raking masts with topsails (*chasse-marées*). Few

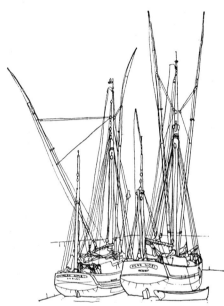

of these are left and have mostly been transferred to the coasting trade.[1] The modern boats are yawl- or ketch-rigged.[2]

The fishing season starts in June and continues until November. From the point of view of colour it would be hard to beat the picturesqueness of the Breton tunny fleet. Their hulls are painted every imaginable shade of green, blue, red, white, and grey. It is seldom that one comes across a boat whose sails are of the same colour: she may have a yellow mainsail, blue topsails, and every shade of brown and red for her mizen and head sails. Even on the Adriatic it would be hard to beat the gorgeous colour-scheme

TUNNY BOATS AT LE PALAIS, BELLE-ILE

presented by these Breton "thonniers" when massed together in the harbour of Concarneau.

Each boat carries two long booms, or fishing-rods, of about the same length as the mainmast, carried on either side of it. These booms can be lowered to almost any position by means of tackle, and are kept taut by being attached forward on either side.

Each of these fishing-rods (*tangons*) carries six lines. They are made of strong hemp, with four or five metres of copper wire at the ends, fastened to which is a bunch of maize straw and horsehair, and a strong, double-ended hook.

[1] See illustration, p. 197.   [2] See also illustration, p. 181.

Between the first and third lines there are also two other lines fixed on to the *tangons*, called *hâle-à-bords*, to haul in the fish near without disturbing the other lines. At the stern of the boat, attached to the mizen, should the craft be ketch-rigged, are two more lines.

The fishing is carried on while the boat is sailing at a speed of four or five knots. The bunches of maize jump about on the surface of the water, the tunny leap after them, swallow the hook,

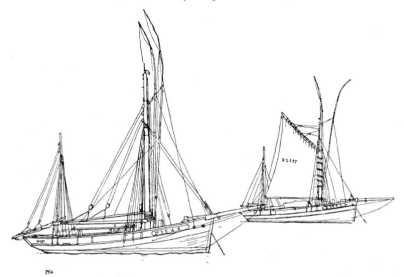

TUNNY BOATS AT DOUARNENEZ

and are hauled in on board. The tunny struggles violently when hauled in, sometimes wounding the men. Many of them wear gloves. The fish is killed by piercing its head. They are immediately cleaned, washed, and hung up on the wooden frames amidships. Up to the present, efforts to preserve the tunny in ice have not been successful. Until some method can be devised the fishing will always be uncertain, as after every trip much of the catch has to be thrown away.

During the time they are at sea the crew keep four-hour watches, except during the run home, when the watches are eight hours.

At night time the boat is kept close hauled, so as not to get far away from the fishing-grounds. The tunny boats are generally at sea about a fortnight or three weeks, according to the weather.

The conditions of life on board a "thonnier" are better than those on a "sardinier." The crew provide their own food. At 6 a.m. there is a *petit déjeuner* consisting of coffee and bread and butter. At midday a substantial dinner of *soupe de poisson*, made of the livers and hearts of the tunny, or else a *ragoût*, served with potatoes and vegetables. Two glasses of wine per head are allowed to each man. At 6 p.m. there is supper, *ragoût de thon* being a staple dish, varied by grilled tunny. Later on a brew of strong tea is served out.

As a general rule the owner of the boat provides all the gear with the exception of the hooks, which are paid for out of a special 'fund called a *total*, contributed equally by the owner and the crew, which also pays for the food of the men when they are in port.

As soon as the fish has been sold and the *total* deducted, the amount is divided into ten or eleven parts. The crews are paid on a share basis. The captain receives two shares, each man one share, the *mousse* a half-share. The remainder belongs to the owners. In some cases the captain is the owner of the boat. On a large "thonnier" the crew consists of five men, the captain, and *mousse*, making a total of seven. On the smaller and older boats the total number of the crew is seven.

It is an interesting sight to watch the tunny being landed at Concarneau on the return of a boat from the fishing. The fish are taken down off the racks, where they have been hung up under canvas awnings to keep them from the sun and rain, dropped overboard into *canots* lying alongside, and rowed ashore to the quays. The blue-grey silvery fish, with their dangerous-looking fins and tails, are then piled up on motor lorries and hurried off to the factories, where they are treated in much the same way as sardines.

The fish are sold by the dozen, but when they weigh less than five kilograms they are sold in pairs. Under 3.500 kilograms they are classed as *bonita*, and are not paid for at the same rates.

The prices given vary enormously according to the season, a serious matter both for the fisherman and for the curer, as it is impossible to reckon expenses before the beginning of the year's fishing.

The rapid increase in the tunny fisheries during the present century has been a source of great commercial prosperity to the inhabitants of Concarneau, Douarnenez, Lorient, Groix, and Auray, which are the chief ports engaged in the industry.[1]

The greater number of tunny fishermen are drawn from the Ile-de-Groix, which has the honour of having introduced this kind of fishing to Brittany. But Concarneau possesses a larger fleet of boats.

[1] Number of tunny boats fishing out of the following Breton ports in 1929: Camaret 4, Crozon 4, Douarnenez 80, Audierne 1, Guilvinec 1, Loctudy 3, Concarneau 123, Port-Louis 82, Groix 198, Etel 141, Quiberon 1, La Trinité-sur-Mer 1, Ile-aux-Moines 6.

CHAPTER VIII

TYPES OF FISHING VESSELS AND OTHER CRAFT ON THE COAST OF BRITTANY

BEFORE starting to write about the different types of fishing vessels and other boats to be found on the coast of Brittany, I must confess, that like every one else who has attempted a survey of these Breton craft, I found it practically impossible to obtain definite information in most of the ports. "The Breton boat-builder is almost as deficient in business instinct as his Cornish cousin. His yard is difficult, often dangerous, of access; his handwriting is illegible, and never can he tell you anything you want to know. 'C'est comme ceci . . . monsieur'—'It be this way, sir.' You are no forrarder after an hour of talking." [1] This was Captain Leslie Richardson's experience after several years spent among the Breton fishermen. My own has been similar. So far as I have been able to discover there are no French books which have attempted to deal with the evolution of the Breton fishing craft. So I regret that the following notes are so superficial. However, I think that my sketches include typical examples of practically all the types of fishing and coasting vessels that are found between Saint-Malo and Saint-Nazaire.

(1) *Plats* (pp. 3, 141, 144).[2] These three sketches made on the Ile-d'Ouessant give a good idea of the lines of these curious little boats, probably the most primitive sort of craft left on the coast of Brittany. They are not far removed from the coracles in which the sailor-monks, Brendan, Samson, Pol de Léon (to mention but a few), ventured across the ocean from Ireland or South Wales during the sixth century. They are not much more than four or five feet in length, and roughly built with planks nailed on to a wooden framework. In drawings on pp. 141, 144 you see the "plats" drawn up on the beach in the creek at Porz-Kinzy, Ouessant. Notice how

---

[1] Cf. *Yachting Monthly*, January 1913.   [2] The numbers refer to illustrations.

OLD TYPE OF FISHING BOATS AT DOUËLEN

they are carried down to the water: the oar being used as a sort of handle. Sometimes the men actually fish from these tiny little craft. More often, however, they merely use them to row out to their larger boats which are left over night at their moorings.

The letters "LC" painted on *Saint-Jean* (p. 3) indicate the port of Le Conquet.

(2) *Small open boats*, used for lobster, crab, and line fishing off the north coast of Finistère and adjacent islands. Typical examples of these craft will be noticed in illustrations on pp. 55, 131, 141, 144. Their characteristic features are their great beam, raking stern, and straight stem. They are almost flat-bottomed and with an average over-all length of 20 ft. Their normal rig is a gaff and boom mainsail, jib, and foresail. Sometimes they carry a topsail. They are roughly built, having the look of a child's first efforts in making a model boat! As a general rule the hull is tarred. This is the type of boat in ordinary use from Argenton to Roscoff (e.g. Lanildut, Argenton, Porspoder, Porsal, Aberbenoit, Aberwrach, Paluden, Le Corréjou, Kerlouarn, Brignonan, Kernic, Ile-d'Ouessant). A similar type of craft is to be found on the Côtes-du-Nord, e.g. at Ploumanac'h. Fishing is carried on within a comparatively short distance of land.

(3) *Sardine boats*. The earliest type of "sardiniers" were all open boats, and lug-rigged, but within the past thirty years they have been gradually superseded by smacks and motor-driven vessels.[1]

Luggers. The general characteristic features of this type of boat were rough primitive construction, great beam and rake of stern, flat bottom; foremast stepped in the eye of boat,[2] mainmast almost amidships,[3] very lofty peaked sails.

(*a*) The original type—a survival of which can still be seen in the Golfe-du-Morbihan luggers—had a long, straight keel, straight stem, and vertical stern-post. They were very slow under sail.

(*b*) The next stage in the evolution of the sardine boat would appear to be the clipper bow, long overhanging stem, and short keel type of boat, of which very few now remain. During the summer of 1930 I failed to discover any of them, except one boat

[1] See p. 85.   [2] See p. 81.   [3] See p. 175.

at Douëlen (*Marie*, CC 3572), see illustration p. 93. The stern has
a tremendous rake, the foot of the rudder being almost amidships.
Probably there are some of this type of boat left in other out-of-

LOBSTER BOAT AT GUILVINEC (See p. 99)

the-way harbours on the south coast of Brittany, where they are
used for lobster and line fishing.

(*c*) The straight stem and elliptical stern were another stage in
the development of the "sardinier." The shape of the stern varies
considerably—square, pointed, and elliptical being found in boats

of about the same size—as will be seen from the numerous examples given in illustrations on pp. 79, 81, 83, 93, etc.

The larger boats are decked, and remind one of an old Scottish "Zulu," with their immense beam and raking stern, although they are not nearly so low in the water. Their rig consists of two sets of dipping lugs. The sheet of the main- and after-lug is either rove through a block on the rudder head or through a block on the stern-post; an inconvenient arrangement, as it necessitates the tiller being raised up and put outside the sheet whenever the helm is put hard down. The sails are tanned either brown or red.

The hulls are generally tarred, although in certain ports one finds examples of this type of boat painted grey. As in all the Breton boats the name is painted on the quarter (often very difficult to read) and the registered number and port on both sides of the bows in white paint.

Other interesting features are the curious wooden pump, which discharges along a hollow thwart (illustrations, pp. 81, 93), and the coarse and heavy sweeps, kept in a crutch formed out of the forked branch of a tree. The blades of the sweeps are lashed on to a square boom. The nets are kept in a wooden chest fitted into the stern of the boat (illustration, p. 93). There is no cabin; the crew sleep on the bottom boards. Cooking is done with a fire lighted on a flat stone. Stone ballast is carried inside.

Average dimensions of these boats are: length, 50 ft.; beam, 10 ft.; draught, 5 ft. 10 in. They carry a crew of five men.

(d) *Cutter-rigged sardine boats* (illustrations, pp. 37, 41, 192, 201). At a distance these boats might easily be taken for the small beam trawlers or line-boats in use at Le Pouliguen and Le Croisic, or on the north coast of Brittany. Their rig consists of mainsail, topsail, and two headsails. As a general rule their stems are square, but in the larger boats counter stems are found. Occasionally one comes across sharp-pointed sterns, all with a great rake. The long bowsprits are parallel to the water line, in startling contrast to the high sheer of the bows. Roller reefing is used on most of these cutter-rigged "sardiniers," unlike the "thonniers," which have loose-footed mainsails.

The hulls are generally painted black above the water-line, occasionally white, blue, or grey.

The sails are usually tanned brown, but sometimes one notices other colours.

These cutter-rigged "sardiniers" are often away from their home port one or two months during the season. During the winter they are employed for mackerel fishing. The crew consists of five men and a *mousse*.

(4) *Tunny boats.* Tunny fishing was not started on the coast of Brittany much before 1900. The original type of boat employed was the old "chasse-marée" (now practically extinct—see illustration—or relegated to the coasting trade). At the present time the "thonniers" are either yawl- or ketch-rigged: all the modern vessels being large ketches of about the following dimensions: length, 100 ft.; beam, 20 ft.; draught, 8–10 ft. In the older vessels stone ballast was used, in the newer ones iron ballast in cement. Characteristic features of the "thonniers" (see illustrations, pages 21, 63, 88, 89, 181) are the broad, flat, counter sterns, the high sheer in the bows, and the lofty fishing-rods (*tangons*) already described in another chapter. Most of them carry a boomless, gaff-headed mizen, on a long outrigger. Sometimes a balloon jib and mizen topsail are used. A feature of the tunny boats is their loose-footed mainsails. Their bowsprits and mizen outrigger are often topped up when in port, like those of a Thames barge. The hull of a "thonnier" is painted every imaginable colour—white, blue, and grey being the favourites.

Elsewhere I have described the colour-schemes of the canvas.

The boats are very fast and seaworthy, working anywhere between one and two hundred miles off the land. The crew consists of seven men, including the captain and the *mousse*.

A word must be said about the Morbihan luggers. They are of the same build as the earliest type of "sardiniers," but the rig is curious, recalling that of a primitive galley. Each boat carries two tall narrow square-headed lugsails, almost rectangular in shape. The canvas is generally tanned a bright red. They are used in the Golfe-du-Morbihan both for fishing and cargo.

Along the north coast of Brittany the ordinary type of decked fishing-boat in use is a cutter-rigged vessel with a square, slightly raking stern, such as I have sketched in the drawings of Saint-Servan, Le Légué, and Portrieux. A few old two-masted luggers are to be found in out-of-the-way creeks.

The Cancale "bisquines," with their immensely raked stern,

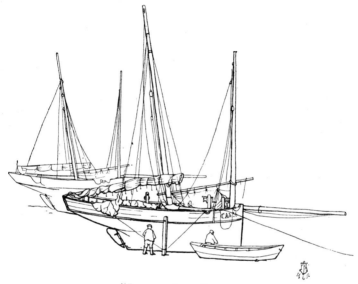

"Bisquines" at Cancale

foremast right in the bow, mainmast amidships, and long bowsprits, still maintain the traditional French lugsail rig that used to be so familiar right down the Channel from the coast of Flanders to Finistère, but which is fast disappearing. In calm weather, in addition to their ordinary lug topsails, the Cancale "bisquines" carry light upper topsails—a marvellous sight. Some typical "bisquines" are shown in the illustration on this page and on p. 105. Average measurements of a Cancale "bisquine" are: length over all, 40 ft.; beam, 10 ft.; draught, 4 ft.; displacement 15–20 tons. The total sail area is about 500 ft.

The crabbers ("langoustiers") may be divided roughly into two classes:

(*a*) Larger boats: ketch rig, with counter sterns, great beam, high bows, and deep draught; average length about 50 ft. over all.

(*b*) Smaller boats: pole mast, cutter rig with square-headed topsail and roller reefing on mainsail, raking transom sterns; length about 35 ft. over all. Crew in both cases, five men.

Typical examples of both these types are to be seen in the drawings of Loguivy, Camaret, and Guilvinec (pages 95, 100, 129, 165, 176).

The Breton crabbers fish chiefly off the Land's End and Scilly Isles. Their manner of life is described in another chapter.

The "dundees," now used chiefly for coasting trade, but formerly engaged in the Iceland fisheries, are dandy-rigged ketches not unlike the North Sea "Billy Boy" or Baltic "Dandy." [1]

Another interesting type of craft is the Brest pilot-boat, of which I regret I was unable to secure a drawing. They are pole-mast cutters, with straight bow, counter stern, and considerable sheer, very fast and seaworthy. Their average length is about 40 ft. over all.

The Rade de Brest is also the home of some sturdy little luggers which carry a light running bowsprit and jib. This distinguishes them from the Concarneau, Audierne, and Douarnenez luggers, which seldom use a bowsprit and jib.

The famous "terre-neuvas" of Saint-Malo, Saint-Servan, and Cancale (the only Breton ports still fitting out vessels for the Newfoundland cod fisheries) are all barquentine rigged, ranging between two and four hundred tons, fitted with roller reefing gear and auxiliary motors. In 1929 sixty-three of these "voiliers" left Saint-Malo for the Newfoundland fisheries. Their number decreases every year. Typical examples are shown in the frontispiece and in the illustrations on page 68.

The "goëlettes" of Paimpol are two-masted schooners engaged in the Iceland and Greenland cod fisheries and coastal trade (see illustration on page 13). They have single square topsails on the fore, with roller reefing gear. In 1929 there were only eleven of

[1] See p. 124.

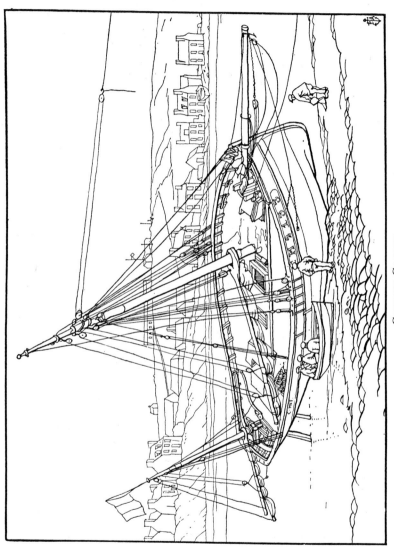

CAMARET CRABBER

these schooners fitted out from Paimpol for the fisheries. They average 180 tons and carry a crew of some twenty-five men. Details of the Iceland fisheries are given elsewhere.

Of the steam and motor vessels found belonging to the Breton ports, there are the recently built motor schooners, one of which is shown in my drawing of Roscoff (p. 137), which are engaged in the coasting trade, and the steam trawlers ("chalutiers") for the Newfoundland, Greenland, and Iceland fisheries.

Téméraire (Saint-Servan), 965 tons (p. 75), is a fine example of these magnificent vessels that are equal, if not superior, to any British steam trawlers.[1] They now number six all told, but more are being built every year. They carry a crew of some fifty men.

[1] The average size of a modern British trawler is between two and three hundred tons.

CHAPTER IX

THE coast of Brittany has no startling or definite natural feature as its starting-point. Gazing landwards from a boat in the great bay of Mont Saint-Michel it is difficult to say precisely where Normandy ends and where Brittany begins. In front is a long, flat shore protected by a dyke. Behind the dyke, marsh lands stretch away inland for many miles. To the westward is a small isolated hill, Mont Dol; the first impression is that it must be an island like its neighbour Mont Saint-Michel. This lonely hill stands like a sentinel keeping guard at the gateway of Brittany, watching over its destinies.

But the actual boundary line of Brittany is the River Couesnou, which flows into the sea to the south-east corner of the bay of Mont Saint-Michel. Once upon a time, the probable date being the year 709, some sudden inrush of the sea took place. Many miles of wooded country and several villages were destroyed and a new coastline was formed. At low tide in the bay of Mont Saint-Michel you can still see the remains of tree-trunks among the sand and mud. During the Middle Ages several attempts were made to reclaim this flooded area, and gradually they succeeded. The rich pasture lands, to-day known as the Marais-de-Dol, are the result. Mont Dol, which for several centuries was an island, is an island no more; it is surrounded by a vast plain and marshes.

The frontier post on the Breton coast is the little village of *Chertrieux*, a hamlet of fishermen, twelve kilometres to the west of the mouth of the Couesnon. Its inhabitants worship in a church whose nave is built in the shape of an upturned ship.

The first real port is *Le Vivier*, a remote little place on the edge of the marshes in a landscape that suggests Holland. A sleepy little place where only a few coasting vessels put in from time to time for the exportation of vegetables and wheat. There are oyster-beds too, and a certain amount of fishing is carried on, but Le Vivier is of small importance commercially. Farther west are the villages of *Hirel* and *Ville-la-Marine*. About eight or nine kilometres beyond we come to the much better-known port of Cancale.

Cancale is a prosperous little town, or, to be more exact, a large, straggling village. Its maritime quarter is called La Houle and lies some distance away from Cancale itself. It consists of a few streets and rows of fishermen's houses "below the brae," as one would say in Scotland. Indeed, Cancale, unlike the majority of Breton fishing-centres, reminds one of some of the ports on the east coast of Scotland. The origin of the settlement is uncertain. It is usually held that the first inhabitants to settle here were refugees from the villages of Porspican and Thomen, which were overwhelmed by the sea in 709. After the eleventh century Cancale was dependent on the Abbey of Mont Saint-Michel, and on more than one occasion it was attacked by the British. In 1758 the Duke of Marlborough and his fleet bombarded the port, and an English squadron sailed into the bay in 1779, firing upon the town.

The Cancale fishermen are of quite a different type from any other seafarers in Brittany. They are strong and well built, and suggest Norse ancestry rather than Celtic. For centuries they have lived for nothing else but the sea; in every sense of the phrase, "the sea is in their blood," and always has been. The majority of Cancale boys go to sea as soon as they leave school, either as *mousses* in a "terre-neuvas" or on board a cargo-boat. Then follow a few years of service in the *marine de guerre*, and at the age of twenty-five or so they return to their former life, either becoming Newfoundland fishermen or rejoining the mercantile marine. They marry, become fathers of large families, and are seldom at home for more than four months in the year. During the summer Cancale seems to be inhabited mostly by women, children, and old men. All the other male population is away at sea. When they get too old for the *Terre-Neuve* fisheries, the Cancalais settle down at home and spend the latter part of their lives as near the sea as possible. Many of them earn a living by fishing in home waters. Others you will find lounging about the harbour and along the quays: veritable *loups de mer*—wolves of the sea!

The port of Cancale is situated in a bay facing almost due east. For this reason it is absolutely sheltered from the prevailing west winds. Further protection is afforded by a stone pier, prolonged by a wooden jetty, known as the Quai-de-la-Fenêtre. At low water the harbour is almost dry, except at the end of the piers. At the south end of the port another pier has been built. Two mooring chains with buoys are laid across the harbour. Vessels can be made fast to these with their stern towards the shore, as will be seen from the accompanying drawing. To the north of the harbour lie the famous Cancale oyster-beds, occupying several acres of water.

During the eighteenth century the mariners of Cancale were famous all over the world. They sailed to the Indies, to America, and Madagascar. Hundreds of dare-devil young Cancalais became corsairs. Many a Cancale seaman ended his days in British prisons during the Napoleonic wars. Under Louis XIV and his successor we read of ships in the navy whose entire crews were drawn from this little port overlooking the bay of Mont Saint-Michel.

Devotion and piety are equally characteristic traits in the Cancalais as bravery and hardiness. A large Calvary stands in a central position right on the seashore close to the harbour. But if you want to understand something of the hold that the Catholic religion still maintains on the majority of Cancale seamen, you must follow them in procession to the shrine of Notre-Dame du Verger, soon after the fishing-fleet has returned home in the autumn from across the Atlantic. Communism and militant socialism have not the same favour here as at Douarnenez and Audierne. The Cancalais is of a more balanced temperament than the fisherman of Finistère. He does not rush from one extreme to another quite so readily. He takes a more placid view of life, even though in character and manners he is spontaneous, genial, and often demonstrative.

Of the famous "bisquines" of Cancale I have written more fully in another chapter. They are far and away the most beautiful

Cancale Harbour: Low Tide

craft to be found anywhere on the coast of Brittany. The local fisheries are very prosperous. Every sort of fish is caught off this stretch of coast and across the mouth of the bay of Mont Saint-Michel, especially mackerel.

But to the majority of Frenchmen the word "Cancale" suggests oysters, just as "Colchester" does to Englishmen. It is worth while to come here during the second fortnight of April in order to witness the famous *caravane*, or annual oyster fishing, the actual date of which is fixed by the Préfet Maritime. Several hundred boats take part in the *caravane*, and the whole business has to be conducted according to a fixed programme. At dawn the firing of a gun gives the signal for the fishing to start. The fleet of boats gets under way immediately, setting their course towards the grounds where the oysters are found. All day long the fishing continues. When the tide begins to rise in the afternoon the fleet returns. Some of them may have two or three hundred oysters on board. On arriving at the beds, the oysters are thrown overboard, each man knowing exactly where his own special "preserve" lies. The cliffs and jetty are crowded with spectators, eagerly watching to see how many fish each boat has on board. The following day at low tide men and women go out to the beds to separate the oysters according to their size. They have to remain on the beds two or three years before they can be sold.

Some four kilometres beyond Cancale, on the north-west side of the Pointe-du-Grouin, from which there is a wonderful view as far as Cap Fréhel in one direction with Mont Saint-Michel and Granville in the other, lies the pilgrimage chapel of Notre-Dame du Verger. Its origins are lost in antiquity, but we know for certain that there was a chapel here as early as the tenth century. It is possible that it was built in thanksgiving for escape from ship-wreck, but no one can say for certain. All that we do know is that seafarers have loved this little shrine of the Blessed Virgin for over a thousand years. The original building was destroyed at the time of the French Revolution. The present church only dates from 1832, and was reconstructed in 1868. Standing remote from any village, within sight and sound of the waves, no more ideal setting could be imagined for a shrine of Our Lady, Star of the Sea. A humble and lowly sanctuary, boasting no beauty of architecture, nor definite historic association, yet beloved by every man, woman, and child of Cancale. They come here in every great moment of their lives. A mother will make a pilgrimage to Notre-Dame du Verger before or after the birth of her child; young lads put up a candle before her image ere they set sail for their first voyage across the Western Ocean. They revisit the chapel to say a prayer of thanksgiving on their return home in the autumn. Indeed no event in the life of a pious Cancalais sailor is complete without the intervention of Our Lady of the Orchard.

The École de Pêche, or Fishery School, founded a good many years ago by one of the local priests, is another feature of the maritime life of Cancale which must not be overlooked. Housed in convenient quarters in a large roomy building behind the new parish church, it has done much to educate the young fishermen and to give them a more intelligent interest in their craft. They are coached here for examinations, they are taught navigation and the working of motor engines. There is a library filled with all the latest technical books. There is no other fishery school to compete with it in France, and the services it renders have been justly recognized by the Government.

Between the Pointe-du-Grouin and Saint-Malo the coast is low and rocky. Not far from the village of *Le Guimorais* lies the house of Jacques Cartier, the discoverer of Canada. We pass *Rothéneuf* and *Paramé*, both on the sea, but having little or no "maritime" character, being popular bathing resorts.

Saint-Malo. Most of us get our first impression of Saint-Malo from the deck of the steamer after a night's voyage from Southampton. There could be no better way of approaching this "city of corsairs," for it enables one to appreciate its true character as the home of a race of seafarers for over a thousand years. One beholds a low, long, fortified town rising out of the water, surrounded by immensely thick walls of sombre grey granite, above which are piled up grey granite houses with high-pitched roofs and great stacks of chimneys. The whole thing is somehow suggestive of a powerfully armed galleon or three-decker, the slender spire of the cathedral taking the place of a mast. It must have been a formidable place to attack. One understands why it was never captured by the English. The more you see of Saint-Malo, the more often you want to return to it and the more you feel how utterly it belongs to the sea.

Thirteen hundred years ago there were no houses where the city now stands, only a bare inhospitable rock partly surrounded by water. On this rock dwelt a hermit called Aaron. One day a little boat landed on the shore. In it were some Celtic monks who had sailed across the Channel from South Wales to escape the ravages of the dreaded Norsemen, who were laying waste and pillaging Britain at that time. Among them was Saint Maclou, or Malo, who on the death of Aaron became abbot of the community of solitaries who lived on this sea-girt rock facing the ocean. Later on he was consecrated Bishop of Aleth, the Gallo-Roman town situated where is now Saint-Servan. Years passed, and Aaron's rock was gradually built over. Aleth declined, and in 1144 the bishopric was transferred to what is now called Saint-Malo. Even in those far-off days the inhabitants of this city were famous as seafarers: a brave and hardy race of mariners who owed allegiance to no sovereign save their bishop. They proudly claimed they were subject to no earthly monarch, and respected none save the successor of Peter the Fisherman. They refused to submit to the Duke of Brittany. Their city was besieged and eventually fell before superior forces. No doubt, had the attack been made by sea, the Malouins would have been victorious, but they were not accustomed to fight on dry land. Nevertheless they continued to be more or less independent. They lived apart from the rest of Brittany, shutting themselves up behind their thick walls of granite. They took no part in the Wars of Succession. They did not bother themselves about kings and princes. They had the sea and their ships, what more did they want? "Ni Français, ni Bretons, Malouins seulement," they proudly boasted. And this is the spirit of Saint-Malo to-day. At the time of the League, Saint-Malo was an independent republic. It was not until 1594 that they were

SAINT-MALO, QUAI SAINT-VINCENT AND LA GRANDE-PORTE

obliged to surrender to Henri IV, and put up with a governor appointed by the king.

During the Hundred Years' War the Saint-Malo ships under Tanneguy and Chatel sailed up the English coast and attacked Great Yarmouth. In the year 1483 it was the Malouins who managed to save Mont Saint-Michel from being captured by the English. Nowadays they fight the English no more. They find it more profitable to make money out of them as tourists and visitors. And they do it so pleasantly, and with such delightful hospitality, that the English do not protest! On the contrary, they return the following year.

The heroic age of Saint-Malo does not really begin until the sixteenth century. It was the discovery of America that gave the Malouins the opportunity which they needed for the full development of their seafaring character. They looked westward across the ocean, dreamed of new lands to conquer, more wealth to be gained. For the next two hundred years there was no busier port in France. Ships were constantly being fitted out. There were fights with the English in the Channel in which the Malouins were generally victorious. There were expeditions to the Arctic, as far north as Spitzbergen. Jacques Cartier discovered Canada. Duguay-Trouin made himself famous on the coast of Brazil. Robert Surcouf is still remembered in Madagascar and in India. Malouin ships and seamen were found in every port of the world. Their flag flew on all the seven seas. Wherever there was fighting to be done, or money to be made by honest trading or legalized piracy, there were the mariners of Saint-Malo.

Jacques Cartier was born in 1491. He is perhaps the greatest of all Malouin sailors. Before his time only Newfoundland and Labrador had been known to Europeans, as the Basques and Bretons had been fishing for cod off these coasts for several hundred years. In 1534 Cartier sailed up the River Saint Lawrence as far as where now stands Quebec. The following summer he returned with three ships, including the *Grande Hermine*, given by François I for the expedition, and arrived at the site of Montreal. It was here that he saw Indians smoking tobacco, an amusing description of which is given in his memoirs: "The Indians," he writes, "possess a certain herb of which they lay in a supply every year after drying it in the sun. Only the men use it. They carry a certain quantity in a little bag that hangs round their neck, in which is also a piece of stone or hollow wood, not unlike a whistle. In order to make use of this herb it is crushed up and placed in the end of the tube, and set alight by means of a piece of hot charcoal. The men breathe up the fumes, filling their lungs so that the smoke escapes from their mouth and nostrils, as it would do from the chimney of a house." No doubt Cartier's sailors experimented with the use of this strange herb that so excited their curiosity, and having found the pleasant and agreeable effect it produced, procured a supply for themselves and thus introduced the practice of smoking to the seamen of Brittany.

I have not the space in this book to tell the story of Jacques Cartier's voyages, of his adventures with the Indians, of his attempts to discover a north-west passage to India. You will find them recorded elsewhere.

Saint-Malo must have been a wonderful place during the seventeenth and eighteenth centuries. The city became more and more prosperous as its maritime trade developed. A contemporary writer tells us that "the Malouins live in splendour and in luxury, fish is very cheap, oysters cost next to nothing, there is excellent waterfowl, and French and Spanish wines, both red and white." He is eloquent on the charms of the Malouine ladies, "most of whom are beautiful, white-skinned, and plump, wearing high-heeled shoes because of their short stature. The men are inclined to be coarse and rough, *moribus maritimis*, but many have travelled, and this has helped to polish up their manners."[1]

It was during this period that were built those stately granite stone mansions, with their steep slate roofs and stacks of chimneys, which greet one when approaching Saint-Malo from the sea. Most of them date from the first quarter of the eighteenth century. In their cellars can be seen remains of old mooring-posts, to which

[1] Dubuisson-Aubenay, *Itinéraire de Bretagne*, 1636; quoted by Étienne Dupont, *Les Corsaires chez eux*, p. 20.

ships were made fast before the erection of the existing quays, the walls on the west of the city being of more recent construction than those to the south and east.   In these vast houses dwelt the rich sea-captains and merchants with their families.   And they needed big houses in those days.   They believed in having as many children as possible, and a family of twenty does not appear to have been anything extraordinary.   They grew rich by means of sea-borne trade, but the principal source of riches was legalized piracy, in other words the fitting-out of privateers.   The only difference between a common "pirate" and a "corsair" consisted in the fact that the latter was supposed to have obtained *lettres de course*, i.e. a commission from the king to harass the seas for the benefit of the State. Each captain was under a certain obligation to present an inventory of what he had captured after every successful voyage, but it seems doubtful if these regulations were strictly complied with!   For a long while the whole business was looked upon with a certain disapproval by the Church.   It was not easy to make it fit in with even the broadest interpretations of moral theology.   But it had become such a normal part of the everyday life of Europe that it was hard to see how it could be essentially wrong.   So the learned doctors came to the conclusion that "all that is taken by force for the benefit of the State is lawful and in accordance with the Divine Law."   The corsairs were satisfied.   Had they not got the Church on their side?   Like the Crusaders of old they could now cry, "Dieu le veut, Dieu le veut," when recruiting a ship for a voyage of plunder. After all, France was at war with England and Holland during most of the seventeenth and eighteenth centuries.   And if any man was scrupulous of his sometimes ill-gotten gains was there not always the old maxim, *Eleemosyna redemit peccatum*?   Many satisfied their consciences with generous gifts to churches, and in more than one place in Brittany you can still see the magnificent altars, chalices, and vestments which were the donation of some pious privateer.   And they *were* pious and devout sons of the Church whatever may have been their deficiences in other directions.   In 1717 a strict rule was made that every ship with a crew of over forty was obliged to carry a chaplain under pain of a fine of not less than two thousand livres. No difficulty seems to have been found in finding priests for this post, for the love of the sea was as strong in the Breton of those days as now. Some of them may not have been remarkable for their priestly character, but the majority seem to have left little to desire in the way in which they discharged their duties, among whom should be mentioned the Franciscan, Père Pelletier, the Benedictine, Dom Sébastien Henry, and the Franciscan, Père Joseph Jeanneau, who was chaplain to the privateer in which Prince Charles Edward escaped from Scotland after the battle of Culloden. But the most famous of all was the Abbé Jouin (1672–1720), whose life and adventures have been told by Monsieur Étienne Dupont in his fascinating book *L'Aumônier des Corsaires* (1926).

There were two classes of vessels engaged in this legalized piracy, the smaller "goëlettes" and "chasse-marées" being built at the shipyards on the Rance, at Saint-Servan, Landriais, and La Richardais, the larger "trois-mâts" being constructed at Lorient, in the yard belonging to the Compagnie des Indes. As a rule no difficulty seems to have been found to get crews for the corsairs, although we hear of certain instances where the press-gang had to be employed, and the aid of a *coup de tikiki*, i.e. a doped glass of wine or *eau-de-vie*. Life was hard and often brutal on board the corsairs, yet things were made easier from the fact that most of the crews were drawn from the same families. We read of more than one instance where the chaplain thought it his duty to interfere when a captain had been treating his *mousse* with more than lawful severity, as on a certain occasion when a boy was lashed to the mast by his hands and feet, stripped naked, and ordered to be flogged for some act of disobedience. They were a brave and fearless lot, those privateer captains, although many of them had but little scientific knowledge of seamanship or navigation. It was in order to remedy this state of affairs that the École d'Hydrographie was founded by Colbert at Saint-Malo in 1660.

Interesting details have been preserved regarding the rations served out to the crews of the corsairs. Five days a week they were given either salt beef or pork. *Maigre* was always the rule on Fridays and fast days of the Church. Sometimes dried cod was provided, or, lacking that, sardines and butter. There was wine, cider, and brandy in plenty to make up for the poor quality of the drinking-water, which had to be kept in casks. Illness and disease seems to have been only too common. In quite a number of the larger vessels a doctor was carried as well as a chaplain, so that every provision was made for the bodies as well as the souls of the crews. The scene of most of their piratical exploits were the waters of the English Channel, where vessels richly laden with cargo returning from the West Indies or Africa were nearly always to be met with. Sometimes the corsairs would cruise as far north as the Bristol or Saint George's Channel in search of their prey.

Then, as now, the streets of Saint-Malo seem to have afforded every opportunity for the sailor to indulge in his favourite pleasures when he came ashore after a voyage. In the early part of the eighteenth century there were some fifty *débits* patronized by seamen around the quays of Saint-Malo, apart from the more respectable *hôtelleries* frequented by officers. Many of the *cabarets* and *débits* were kept by Irishmen, notably the "Belle Anglaise," where the *patronne*, one Margaret Collins, seems to have more than once got into trouble with the police for the character of her establishment. Vice may have been coarse and brutal in those bygone days, but the civil authorities of Saint-Malo took care that it was kept within certain limits, and the *filles de joie* were strictly forbidden to "*extravaguer* [*sic*] sur le port," to wander round the cathedral, and in the streets frequented by honest persons. If they were discovered out of doors later than 9 p.m. they were sent to prison or to hospital.

Owing to the heavy taxation of tobacco, wine, and spirits by the Government, also the poor quality of the State tobacco, large quantities of these articles were smuggled into Saint-Malo during the eighteenth century, so that smuggling became almost as common as piracy, and as recognized a profession. Gambling among the richer classes reached an alarming development during this period of prosperity, fortunes were made and lost within a few days. What did it matter when there was always the chance of capturing a rich English vessel a few miles off in the Channel?

They were a rough lot, these old privateers, living their lives to the full, with their virtues as well as their vices; pious and devout in their own way, good sons of the Church, in spite of what would now be called the more or less piratical nature of their career. But times were different, and it is not fair to judge them by twentieth-century standards. We can respect them as one of the finest races of seamen Europe has ever produced, and of whose valour France may well be proud, and whose spirit is kept alive in the present-day *Terre-Neuvas*, of whom I have written in another chapter.

Saint-Malo really forms a common port with Saint-Servan, although each place possesses its own quays and basins. Both are protected by a number of outlying islands and rocks, of which Cézembre is the largest. Between the two was formerly a swampy marsh, now reclaimed. A stone jetty, the Mole-des-Noires, defends both ports from the north-east winds. The *Port d'Échouage*, where the Southampton and Jersey steamers are berthed alongside the Quai Saint-Vincent, is dry at low water. The wet dock is surrounded by quays on three sides. On the east side are shipbuilding yards. It is entered from the *Port d'Échouage* by a lock, closed by four pairs of gates. The entrance to the wet dock at Saint-Servan is at the west by means of a lock. Saint-Servan has another harbour.

CHAPTER X

AFTER leaving Saint-Malo there is no port of any real importance until we reach Saint-Brieuc. *Dinard* and *Saint-Lunaire* are nothing more than fashionable *plages*, crowded with bathers during the summer, somewhat deserted in winter. *Saint-Brieuc*, named after an Irish monk, was formerly a fishing-village with a large fleet of boats. The apsidal chapels of the old parish church have some curious stone carvings of mackerel, offerings of fishermen in bygone days. This port dries at low water, is difficult to enter in bad weather, and has now scarcely any trade. Just beyond Saint-Brieuc one enters the *département* of the Côtes-du-Nord.

Farther west, on the opposite side of the Baie de Lancieux, lies the port of *Saint-Jacut-de-la-Mer*, another fishing-village that has greatly decreased in importance and which is fast becoming a popular watering-place. There is a small harbour protected by a mole.

Le Guildo is a small port on the estuary of the Arguenon where boats generally anchor while waiting for the tide to take them to *Plancoët*, three miles farther inland, a sleepy little place, with scarcely any maritime trade. *Saint-Cast* is rapidly changing its character from a primitive fishing village to a fashionable and select *plage*. The Port de Saint-Cast consists of a natural bay with a small pier. Not far from here is an ancient chapel dedicated to Saint Blanche, formerly much frequented by sailors and fishermen. At the far end of the Baie de la Frénaye, which affords complete shelter from all winds except the north-east, is another tiny little port, *Port-Nieux*, with a short quay alongside which you will sometimes come across an occasional "dundee" or smack.

Between the Baie de la Frénaye and Erquy, we round the famous headland *Cap Fréhel*, with its lighthouse and signal station, a popular excursion from all the neighbouring seaside resorts on account of its fine cliff scenery. Seamen, on the contrary, look upon Cap Fréhel as a place to avoid. It is surrounded by dangerous rocks, and owing to the strong tides and heavy breaking seas found there in certain winds, vessels give it a wide berth.

About fifteen kilometres west of Cap Fréhel lies the fishing village of *Erquy*, like most of its neighbours developing into a summer resort with a *syndicat d'initiative*, and fast losing its primitive character. At one time Erquy used to fit out vessels for the Newfoundland cod fisheries. Its seamen were famous all along the coast. In the little harbour, dry at low water, and sheltered by a stone jetty, there is always a certain amount of activity: vegetables, especially potatoes, are exported to England, and a regular trade is done by shipping stone from the quarries on the cliffs for use in pavements. Just beyond the *plage* of Val-André is another little tidal port, *Dahouët*, picturesquely situated, but seldom frequented, and quite impracticable in north-west winds, owing to its exposed position.

None of these places between Saint-Malo and Saint-Brieuc which I have mentioned have any importance either commercially or as regards fishing. But in all of them you will find a population of seafarers, varying in number according to the size of the village. Some of the men are engaged in fishing, some are in the merchant service, others in the navy. It would be scarcely worth while to refer to them, except that in a study of maritime Brittany their names at least must be given.

The Baie de Saint-Brieuc is the largest inlet on the north coast of Brittany. Its area has been greatly increased within the last two thousand years owing to the encroachments of the sea. The coastline has changed, and at low tide one now finds immense stretches of sand, where in the time of the Romans existed forests and cultivated land.

Saint-Brieuc itself has nothing maritime about it, except its origin. The city is named after a Celtic monk who sailed across from Ireland or South Wales some time during the fifth century, accompanied by a band of disciples. They are supposed to have landed at the mouth of the River Gouët. Saint Brieuc preached

Christianity all through the surrounding country, performed extraordinary miracles, and after his death was buried on the site of the present cathedral.

The port of Saint Brieuc is situated four kilometres outside the city, in a deep valley shut in by steep hills. It is known as *Le Légué*: a sleepy, abandoned sort of place that has known much greater prosperity than at present. There are two basins, the old and the new: the former bordered by grass-grown quays nearly two thousand feet in length, where half a century ago you would have found a fleet of "goëlettes" and other sailing craft. Nowadays there seems to be very little activity. Le Légué is a somewhat depressing spot. Beyond the old basin, nearer the sea, is the new basin, built on the site of the old grounding port. At one time Le Légué was among the chief ports for fitting out vessels for the Newfoundland cod fisheries. To-day it is only frequented by English colliers, Scandinavian timber ships, and small cargo vessels which export vegetables and agricultural produce to England.

At the mouth of the River Gouët, two kilometres beyond Le Légué, is the fishing village of *Sous-la-Tour*, opposite the wooded hill of Le Cesson, surmounted by an old ruined tower, conspicuous for a long distance out to sea. Ship lovers should make a point of visiting Sous-la-Tour. They will find many an old type of sailing craft, now practically extinct, lying rotting on the shore. The fishermen who still practice their craft in the sort of boats I have sketched in the drawing on p. 31 are a friendly lot, and one can spend many an amusing hour chatting with them as they mend their nets or work on their boats. There are restaurants where a cheap and excellent meal can be had; there is a beautiful view across the bay of Saint-Brieuc. Taken in all there are many worse places on the north coast of Brittany!

Fourteen kilometres north of Saint-Brieuc one comes to *Binic*, a place of importance in the maritime history of Brittany, for it was from this little port that the first vessel was fitted out for the Newfoundland cod fisheries. Up to that time the fishing had been controlled by the Basques; Breton seamen working on board Basque ships as part of the crew. *Bénicasser la morue*—the name given in

BINIC

the sixteenth century to a certain method of curing codfish—is derived from the word Binic.

Binic, a quiet, peaceful village of some two thousand inhabitants, has a population made up of sailors and others whose business is more or less directly connected with the sea and ships. During the summer months most of its menfolk are away on the Grands Bancs, and its streets and long quays seem strangely deserted, although no vessels are actually fitted out here any more. Of course there are women and children: swarms of the latter, as in every fishing village all the world over.

In the great, spacious church, whose spire you will notice in the illustration, is an elaborate high altar in white marble that seems rather out of place here in the grey granite of Brittany. It came from Marseilles, presented to the church by the *Terre-Neuvas* of Binic, who generally sold their fish at Marseilles before returning home in the autumn.

The religious character of the sailors of Binic has always been remarkable. Their devotion expresses itself chiefly in a great devotion to Notre-Dame de la Cour, whose exquisitely beautiful flamboyant Gothic sanctuary is situated about six kilometres inland. It is one of the loveliest examples of late Gothic work to be found anywhere in Brittany; an old weather-beaten chapel of grey granite lying in the midst of low hills, rich meadows, and peaceful valleys. In one of the windows are represented scenes recording the miraculous intervention of Our Lady on behalf of sailors: the model of a great three-masted ship hangs as an ex-voto from the roof before the quaint medieval image of the Blessed Virgin and her Child, above the high altar. On the Feast of the Assumption, 15th August, crowds come here for the annual Pardon, conspicuous among whom are seamen with their wives and families. On such an occasion one realizes what a hold the Catholic religion still maintains in the heart of the mariners of Brittany, despite unceasing efforts to suppress it.

The harbour of Binic is situated at the mouth of the little river Ic. It consists of an *avant-port* and inner harbour, with an opening to the eastward. Good shelter is afforded in south and westerly

PORTRIEUX

winds, but when the wind is from the north and east the place is much exposed. The *avant-port* is surrounded by the moles of Pordic and Penthièvre, and like the inner harbour is almost dry at low water. Apart from the cod fisheries there is not much commerce at Binic. A few small cargo-boats put in here from time to time to export vegetables, and a certain amount of trawl fishing is still carried on.

Ten kilometres north of Binic, we come to yet another little harbour, *Portrieux*, which is more sheltered than the former. There is a good anchorage, protected by a stone jetty, alongside which small craft can be moored, even at low tides. The fisheries of Portrieux are of considerable importance, boats from as far off as Douarnenez landing their fish here occasionally. Many of the local seamen are engaged in the Newfoundland cod fisheries. In bygone years it was a common sight in winter to see the wooden "terre-neuvas" moored bows on to the beach, their sterns secured by chains. The Rade de Portrieux, offshore, affords a good anchorage, and is much used by vessels waiting for the tide to take them into Binic, Dahouët, or Le Légué.

Plouëzec, *Plouha*, and *Kérity* are not seaports, but boast a population almost entirely made up of seafarers, most of whom are engaged in the *Terre-Neuve* or Iceland fishing. Not far from Plouëzec is the little harbour of *Port-Lazot*, where there are oyster-beds and a small fleet of fishing-boats.

The town of *Paimpol* is situated at the head of a bay three miles across at its entrance, between the Pointe de la Trinité and the Pointe de Plouézec. A narrow tongue of land, the Pointe de Guilben, divides the bay into two parts. On its north side lies the port of Paimpol. It is sheltered from almost every wind, and at Paimpol itself one is quite out of sight of the open sea.

The port consists of an *avant-port* and two wet docks; the former connected with the *bassin-neuf* by a lock, the *vieux-bassin* opening out of the latter on the south-east. There are spacious quays on either side of the *avant-port* which immediately faces the business quarter of the town. Apart from the Iceland fisheries not much trade is carried on here, except importing coal and timber, and the export of a certain amount of agricultural produce. Indeed, during the summer months, when the fleet of "goëlettes" is away off Iceland, Paimpol is a very sleepy little place, with hardly any visible sign of maritime activity, except perhaps for the presence of the young students at the Sea School being trained as officers for the mercantile marine.

Its history is devoid of any startling events, and the town itself, although it contains some picturesque old houses and is surrounded by pleasant country, has nothing very attractive about it. The old church has been pulled down, only the tower remaining, and the large new church is a typical example of a thousand other nineteenth-century Gothic parish churches anywhere in France, that give one the impression that they must have been designed in the office of some Parisian architect without the slightest reference to the locality in which they were to be erected.

To-day the Paimpol Iceland fisheries are not what they were before the war. In 1929 only eleven schooners were fitted out— seven for Iceland, four for Greenland—a sad decline from the years gone by, when fifty or sixty of these famous "goëlettes," immortalized by Pierre Loti in his novel *Pêcheur d'Islande*, set sail every February.

Paimpol owes much of its fame to Loti, also to Théodore Botrel, whose song *La Paimpolaise* is known all the world over.

The departure of the Iceland fishermen is no longer the imposing function that Loti describes, although it still retains something of its note of tragic mournfulness. On that day every vessel was solemnly blessed before it left the harbour, for instead of as now, when they leave at odd times during the month of February, they were all towed out on the same day. In honour of the occasion a *reposoir*, always of the same design, in imitation of a grotto with rocks, was erected on the quay, in the midst of which, surrounded by trophies of anchors, oars, and nets, the image of Notre-Dame de Bon Voyage from the parish church stood enthroned: a gentle, placid Virgin, patroness of seafarers, taken down from above her altar. She looked on year after year with the same lifeless expression upon the same scene: "upon those for whom the season would be profitable and upon those who would never return." [1] The Blessed Sacrament, followed by a slowly moving procession of mothers, sweethearts, and wives, was borne around the harbour, where lay all the Iceland schooners decorated with flags. The crews respectfully saluted as the Sacred Host passed by. The priest paused a moment, and raising up the monstrance blessed each vessel in turn.

After the ceremony is over, the fleet departs: the women, old and

PAIMPOL

young, waiting on the quayside with an air of tragic resignation for the worst that may happen. The lock gates open, the "goëlettes" pass out two by two, or four by four, until at last no more remain. They are towed out to the open sea, and disappear from view on the horizon. The surrounding country-side is empty of menfolk and boys: the women await their return six months later.

[1] Loti *Pêcheur d'Islande.*

"Then with the first mists of autumn," writes Loti, "they return home, either to Paimpol itself or to the scattered hamlets of the Pays de Goëlo, to occupy themselves for a while with their families —with making love, and marriage, and births, for nearly always there will be found some little baby boys, who are awaiting their fathers and godparents. For this race of fishermen which Iceland devours can do with many children."

"Then a month or two later, when all the fleet has returned save those which had been lost at sea, the Pardon des Islandais takes place on 8th December, Feast of the Immaculate Conception of Our Lady, Star of the Sea. Under the grey skies of winter, more often than not in an atmosphere of drizzling rain, the crews of the 'goëlettes' gave vent to the pent-up emotions of their six or seven months enforced repression at sea in an outburst of savage enjoyment. But it was a brutal, sullen mirth, with nothing of the natural vivacity and lightheartedness of southern races: rather a challenge to destiny and fate; a wish to forget the hardships and privations of those long weeks of grinding, monotonous toil day after day that they had gone through off Iceland, with its storms of blinding rain and chill winds. They craved nothing better than to feel the grateful warmth of alcohol in their bodies, the rousing of all their dormant physical passions and animal lust, so that they could forget for a time the overhanging menace of another year's fishing before them."[1]

In all those little cafés and *bistrots* that abound in the streets around the quays of Paimpol—queer old houses of granite with overhanging eaves; within low and long, great beams supporting the roof; the white- or cream-washed walls displaying primitive paintings of shipwrecks and storms at sea; a china statuette of the Blessed Virgin standing on a bracket in a corner; a zinc bar and shelves laden with bottles of all shapes, colours, and sizes—you would find crowds of stalwart fishermen drinking and smoking their little black clay pipes with the bowl turned downwards, in an atmosphere of intense heat, clouds of tobacco smoke, a smell of brandy, rum, wine, and cider mingled with that of damp clothes

[1] op. cit. Part I, c. ii.

and sweating humanity, a terrific din of voices, shouting, singing, and talking.   This was how the Paimpolais kept the Pardon of Notre-Dame de Bon Voyage in the olden days.   Fights and brawls were frequent.   To-day things are somewhat quieter, but the spirit of the men remains the same from one generation to another, their way of enjoying themselves similar if not quite so violent as fifty years ago.

From Paimpol one can wander out to the fishing village of *Pors-Even* where Loti wrote *Pêcheur d'Islande.*   The house he occupied is still standing.   On the way one passes the village of *Ploubazlanec,* with its *cimetière des naufragés,* a drawing of which appears on p. 5 —a long row of graves above which one reads the names of countless sailors who have never returned home.   About half a mile beyond Ploubazlanec one comes to the hamlet of *Perros-Hamon,* with its little grey granite church standing in a cemetery, surrounded by a few stunted, wind-blown trees.   The walls of this venerable chapel are mellowed and corroded by age and salt-laden air.   Within the porch, on either side of the doorway, are many tablets recording the names of sailors who have been lost at sea.   And on almost all of them one reads the words: "Perdu en Islande . . . disparu en mer . . . qu'ils reposent en paix."   Little more than boys many of them, to judge by their ages: victims, in the full ripeness of their youth and flower of their manhood, to that cruel deity which every year claims the sacrifice of her human victims.

You can sit down on the stone seat within the porch and con-template these pathetic memorials.   Look at that queer macabre-like skull and crossbones on one of the walls.   Listen to the wind murmuring and sighing in the trees.   Surely it must be the voices of the souls of these young fishermen whose bones lie rotting at the bottom of the ocean within the Arctic Circle, and who ask your prayers.

Continuing your walk, you soon arrive at the village of Pors-Even, with its fishermen's houses scattered over the slopes of the cliff that leads down to the shore where there is a small pier.   You pass on and presently come to a path that leads along the edge of the beach to a solitary chapel standing all by itself.   This is the

PORS-EVEN FROM POINTE-DE-GUILBEN

Chapelle de la Trinité—nowadays sadly neglected, its windows broken and the weeds growing within the joints of its masonry. You will remember that Loti refers to it as the place where Yann came with Gaud after their wedding at Ploubazlanec. Then you climb up a steep path behind the chapel to the top of the cliff, eventually arriving at an ancient granite cross, covered with grey and golden lichen. It was here in the olden days of sail, before the introduction of motor power, that the wives and mothers of the fishermen would come and watch, day after day, for the return of the "goëlettes" from Iceland, straining their eyes with eager longing to catch the first glimpse of them on the distant horizon. And sometimes they waited and watched in vain, for the ship they were looking for would never come back. This old cross "stands as it were on the very edge of this land of seafarers," writes the author of *Pêcheur d'Islande*, "as if to ask grace and to appease that vast, mysterious, moving creature that draws men to itself, and does not allow them to return; keeping in preference the most virile and brave."[1]

The *Ile-de-Bréhat* lies about a mile from the mainland and is generally reached by taking a boat from the Pointe de l'Arcouest, four miles north-east of Paimpol. One lands at the *Port-Clos*, a hamlet of fisherfolk which has now developed into a popular summer resort. Most of the inhabitants of l'île-de-Bréhat follow the sea in some capacity or another, either in the mercantile marine or as fishermen. With an exceptionally mild climate, and sub-tropical vegetation growing out in the open air, and wonderfully picturesque rocky coastline, Bréhat attracts a colony of artists every year. Its history is full of vicissitudes. Again and again we read of the island being attacked by the English. There is a story that on one occasion the bodies of some English invaders were suspended from the sails of one of the windmills that at one time were very numerous here.

Loguivy is a delightful little port facing Bréhat, whose hardy seafaring inhabitants are chiefly engaged in fishing for lobsters and crayfish off the coast of Cornwall. It possesses a sheltered

---

[1] op. cit., Part V, c. vii.

harbour formed of two stone piers.   Just beyond Loguivy, the River Trieux leads up to *Lézardrieux*, where a certain amount of trade is carried on by coasting vessels, many of which at high water proceed ten kilometres farther up the river as far as *Pontrieux*.   Coal and timber are imported; potatoes, grain, and flour being exported to England and other parts of France.

Continuing westwards along the coast, passing that curious rocky

LOGUIVY

peninsula known as the *Sillon de Talbert*, in the neighbourhood of which are two villages, *Pleubian* and *Lanmodez*, most of whose male inhabitants are sailors, we arrive at the River *le Tréguier*, about five miles from whose mouth lies the small port of the same name. Coasting vessels unload cargoes of coal, timber, and cement alongside its quays, and agricultural produce is shipped to England.

Port-Blanc is a picturesque fishing village on the cliffs overlooking the Ile Saint-Gildas, and the more distant Sept Iles.   Its little harbour affords shelter for a fleet of boats, mostly engaged in line-fishing or lobster trapping off-shore. On a rock surmounting the harbour is a statue of Our Lady, close to which lies the ancient chapel of Notre-Dame de Port Blanc, whose Pardon on 8th September attracts vast crowds of fishermen and sailors. The chapel dates from the sixteenth century and contains some curious old images, representing Saint Yves between a rich man and a poor man. Anatole Le Braz, the great authority on Breton folk-lore, used to live at Port-Blanc, and in his works there are many references to the fisherfolk of the neighbourhood.

The cliffs continue in the same direction for about twenty kilometres. Passing the fishing village of *Trestel*—which with its neighbour, *Trévou-Tréguignec*, is the home of innumerable seamen—we reach the Anse de Perros, upon whose westerly shore is situated the port and watering-place of *Perros-Guirec*. There is a spacious harbour here, dry at low water, formed of a long jetty on the east and a short mole to the west. Not much trade is done except importing coal and timber and exporting vegetables and agricultural produce. There are a few small fishing-craft here. Five kilometres beyond Perros-Guirec, passing the fashionable and rapidly developing *plages* of *Trestignel* and *Trestaou*, one comes to that strange bit of coast, strewn with enormous boulders of red granite, half hidden among which lies *Ploumanac'h*, once a secluded hamlet of fisherfolk, but now being transformed into a popular summer resort. My drawing shows some of the boats still found here and groups of typical fishermen embarking from the little jetty. From Ploumanac'h a boat can be taken to the *Sept Iles*. You will find detailed descriptions of *La Clarté*, *Trébeurden*, and all the picturesque features of the romantic coast in any guide-book, so I will hurry on until we reach the mouth of the River Léguer, where there is a delightful and unfrequented port called *Le Yeudet*, whose history goes back more than a thousand years, for it is recorded that the place was destroyed by Danish pirates in 836.

Sailing up the River Léguer, which is almost dry at low water, passing another village called *Loguivy*—an out-of-the-world hamlet of seafarers—after ten kilometres or so one reaches *Lannion*. Scarcely

FISHERMEN AT PLOUMANAC'H

claiming the pretensions of being a seaport in the strict sense of the word, Lannion does a certain amount of maritime trade. Alongside its picturesque quays, backed by rows of plane-trees, old houses, and the grey tower of Saint-Jean du Baly, you will often come across some interesting types of sailing craft; "dundees" and "goëlettes" unloading their cargo with a delightful absence of hurry and rush.

The sea-coast beyond the entrance to the River Léguer is unbroken by any port worth mentioning until we reach *Saint-Efflam*, beyond which is the harbour of *Toul-an-Hery*, at the mouth of the Douron, which forms the boundary between the *départements* of the Côtes-du-Nord and Finistère. There is a little jetty and landing-stage here, but few signs of any activity are apparent.

CHAPTER XI

AFTER crossing the estuary of the little River Douron we leave the *département* of the Côtes-du-Nord for Finistère. About two kilometres beyond stands the fishing village of *Locquirec*, with a pleasant view across the bay towards Saint-Michel-en-Grève. There is always a certain amount of traffic going on in this little port. Sailing-vessels put in here with cargoes of paving stone from quarries in the neighbourhood, and line-fishing is engaged in by the local fishermen.

About fourteen kilometres farther west, just before the coastline turns south at the entrance to the bay of Morlaix, is another fishing village, *Diben*, overlooking the favourite bathing resort of *Trégastel-Primel*, where there is also a small fleet of fishing-boats. Sailing up the wide estuary of the river of Morlaix one notices several little groups of whitewashed houses nestling among the trees : *Térénez*, *Le Dourduff-en-Mer* on the right bank, *Carantec* and *Locquénolé* on the left, all of them with a certain maritime population. Off Carantec lies the *Ile-de-Callot*, with its famous pilgrimage chapel of Notre-Dame des Victoires, dating from the sixth century, in memory of a victory gained over the Norse pirates who were ravaging the coast of Brittany. It is on 15th August that one should make a point of visiting the Ile-de-Callot. Sailors from all round the district come here in hundreds to pay their devotions before the sixteenth-century image of Our Lady enshrined in the chapel.

Morlaix is one of the numerous inland towns of Brittany that carries on a regular sea-going trade, thanks to the tidal river upon which it is situated. When passing through by train and looking down from the lofty viaduct, which I have sketched in my drawing, you will generally notice a few tramp steamers, upon whose sterns either the red ensign, or the flags of Norway, Sweden, and Denmark are flying. For coal from South Wales and Tyneside, also timber from Scandinavia, are the chief imports of Morlaix, while pit-props, slates, and agricultural produce are shipped here either to England or other places in France.

Morlaix is not without a certain amount of maritime interest in its historic past, which goes back to the days of the Romans. It was more than once attacked by an English fleet in the Middle Ages. In 1542 was built the Château du Taureau, on an isolated rock at the entrance to the river, as a special defence against the English fleet.

On the edge of the quays a bust of Charles Cornic (1731–1809), the famous sea-rover and corsair, reminds one that the town numbers not a few seafarers among its population, a proof of which may be had in the cheery crowds of *col-bleus* usually to be found waiting at the railway station *en route* for Brest.

A branch line from Morlaix takes one to Roscoff, passing over the River *la Penzé* with its little port of the same name, boasting a few fishing-craft. *Saint-Pol-de-Léon* can hardly claim any maritime interest, although its suburb of *Penpoul* is a favourite resort of yachtsmen, and is the home of a good few fishermen and seamen.

Roscoff, surrounded by vast fields of onions and other vegetables, is one of the most interesting ports in the whole of Brittany, and for none of them have I a greater affection. It is very old, its history dating back more than a thousand years. It has always been connected with England in one way or another. Sometimes its relations were friendly, sometimes exactly the opposite. In 1404 Jean de Penhoët set sail from Roscoff to attack the English fleet, which he eventually defeated off Pointe Saint-Mathieu. Mary Queen of Scots landed here in 1548, when she was a little girl only five years old, to be espoused to the Dauphin at Morlaix. You can still see the house where she lodged, and the old watch-tower, La Tourelle-de-Marie-Stuart, near which she disembarked, alongside which is the ruined chapel of Saint-Ninian. Two hundred years later another Stuart sovereign landed in Roscoff, but in very different conditions: Prince Charles Edward Stuart, a fugitive from the Battle of Culloden. He had fled from Scotland in a French

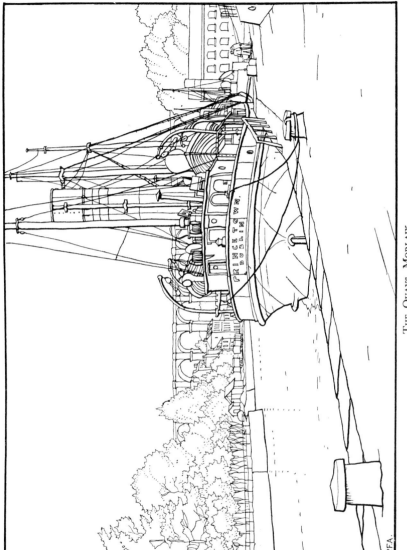

THE QUAYS, MORLAIX

privateer, which only just managed to escape being captured by
the English ships in the Channel. In these days Roscoff does a
busy trade with England all the year round. Little cargo-boats,
either steam, sail, or motor, export vegetables and agricultural
produce to Poole, Southampton, Portsmouth, and Plymouth. Its
tidal harbour, sheltered from all but easterly winds, affords good
anchorage for a fleet of fishing vessels, whose crews are a cheery,
friendly lot, less shy and reserved, and more ready to talk to a
stranger than the majority of Breton sailors. Perhaps that is
one reason why I have such pleasant memories of Roscoff, its
seafarers, and "onion men" (so well known in this country), whose
little port you will see depicted in the drawing on the next page.

From Roscoff one can sail across to the *Ile-de-Batz*, about a mile
to the north, separated from the mainland by a channel in which
the tide flows with extraordinary force.

The Ile-de-Batz is a low, sandy island about four kilometres
long, bordered on all sides by dangerous rocks, the surface is well
cultivated, but the general aspect bare and treeless. Practically
all its male inhabitants (the average population is thirteen hundred)
are seafarers, either in the mercantile marine or engaged in fishing.
The agricultural work on the island is done by women. My drawing
of the island on p. 17 shows some typical fishing-boats lying on the mud
at low tide. In the distance will be noticed the modern church in
the sacristy of which is preserved the stole of Saint Paul Aurelian,
the sixth-century monk, who lived here for some years after he had
sailed across to Brittany from South Wales. Remains of his monas-
tery are still standing on the eastern side of the island.

Some five kilometres to the west of Roscoff lies the *Ile-de-Sieck*,
with a little harbour and a few houses, the former affording shelter
to fishing-boats in easterly gales.

The coastline continues in a westerly direction, broken by
innumerable bays and capes, the shore being low and sandy with
reefs of rocks lying for a considerable distance out to sea. A rather
monotonous coast, not often visited by tourists, but containing a
number of curious and characteristic villages, each with its fleet of
small open boats that fish off the shore, seldom going out of sight

ROSCOFF

of land. Taking them in order the most important are *Kernic,
Brignogan, Kerlouarn, Guissény, Le Corréjou, Paluden,* and *Kéréval.*

The estuaries of *L'Aberwrach* and *L'Aberbenoît* afford safe anchorage
in bad weather, and at one time their little harbours did a considerable export trade in
vegetables and agricultural
produce. But nowadays
they are abandoned and
sleepy.

Off the coast just north
of L'Aberwrach lies the
famous lighthouse of *Ile-
Vierge*: the tallest lighthouse in the world, whose
tower, 225 ft. high, is loftier
than those of Notre-Dame
at Paris.

Porsal, six kilometres
farther west, is another
characteristic fishing centre,
with a sheltered harbour
and a factory for making
iodine from kelp.

Argenton, with a land-
locked harbour, is a busy
little fishing village, so also
is its neighbour *Porspoder*,
two miles beyond which

LE CONQUET

lies *Lanildut*, a small port on the estuary of the Aberildut, frequented
by a few fishing-boats and coasting vessels, and whence stone is
exported from the neighbouring quarries.

All this north-west coast of Finistère has a savage and desolate
aspect. During certain periods of the year the air is heavy with
that curious bitter smell of kelp-burning, the *goëmon* or seaweed
gathered on the rocks being of immense value for making iodine.
If the wind is from the west the dense clouds of smoke blowing over

the rolling landscape, with its scattered whitewashed houses and grey granite spires, remind one sometimes of the forest fires of British Columbia, and it is impossible to escape from the smell of kelp.

Le Conquet is a little seaport town with a venerable past, and whose annals record many a fight with the English; in most of which it was victorious. But in 1558 the English fleet sailed into the harbour, pillaged the town, set fire to the houses, all of which were destroyed except eight, which were spared since they belonged to British subjects. They are still standing as a witness. Le Conquet is well sheltered from the open sea by a stone pier, and still owns a fishing fleet of some importance. Within its modern church lies the tomb of Père Michel le Nobletz, the seventeenth-century priest who devoted his life to the conversion of the seafaring inhabitants of the coast of Finistère and the adjacent islands, the majority of whom up to that time were still little more than pagans. The story of his missionary voyages in open boats, often exposed to the greatest dangers, reads like a romance.

About two miles south of Le Conquet we come to *Pointe Saint-Mathieu*, upon whose rocky cliffs stand the ruins of the Benedictine Abbey founded by Saint Tanguy in the sixth century, and a powerful lighthouse.

Visible to every ship entering the harbour of Brest there has been erected on Pointe Saint-Mathieu a cenotaph-like memorial to the sailors of Brittany who lost their lives during the war, which I have shown in the sketch on page vii. There is something curiously impressive in this huge granite mass surmounted by a sculptured head of a mourning Breton woman, placed on the edge of the cliffs facing the open Atlantic. The view from here is almost more imposing than from the Pointe du Raz farther south. Immediately in front lies the dangerous reef known as the "Chaussée des Pierres-Noires," with its lighthouse. Rather more to the right you have the islands of Béniguet and Molène, while about twelve miles away to the north-west can be made out the island of Ouessant with its two lighthouses. To the south and south-east lies the entrance to the Rade de Brest, the peninsula of Camaret, the curious rocks known as the Tas de Pois, Cap de la Chèvre; and if it is clear enough, the far-distant Pointe du Raz and the lighthouse on the Ile-de-Sein.

CHAPTER XII

FROM Le Conquet one can take the steamer, that starts from Brest twice a week, weather permitting, for the islands of Molène and Ouessant, a passage of two or three hours, or longer according to wind and tide. If you are a bad sailor, do not venture on this trip, for it is seldom that the little *Enez Eussa* does not roll and pitch, with disastrous effects for most of her passengers. But on the other hand you cannot pretend to have more than a superficial knowledge of maritime Brittany unless you have been to Molène and Ouessant, where the soul of the Breton seafarer is revealed to one as nowhere else. It is difficult not to exaggerate the fascination of Ouessant if one happens to be a lover of islands. On no other island in the Atlantic that I am acquainted with—and I admit to having visited most of the Hebrides, Orkneys, and Shetlands—does one realize the tremendous force of the sea, and the brutal strength of the Western Ocean. One leaves the harbour of Le Conquet, steams across the Chenal du Four, where the tide swirls and boils with alarming effect. Soon one passes near to the *Ile Béniguet*, low and forbidding. On every side cruel-looking rocks rise out of the sea, waiting there as if to lure some unfortunate vessel to destruction. After threading a course through their midst, the steamer drops anchor in the harbour of the *Ile Molène*. This desolate-looking island, not more than sixty feet above sea-level at its highest point, and less than half a mile long, has a population of nearly seven hundred, all of whom are fisherfolk. There are no hardier or more daring seamen around the coast of Brittany than those of Molène. Its harbour—well sheltered from the south and west—generally contains a good number of sturdy little schooner-rigged fishing-boats. Lobsters and crab are especially plentiful in the neighbouring waters. To English visitors the chief interest of Molène is connected

Ouessant: Phare de Créach

with the wreck of the liner *Drummond Castle*, which ran aground on the reefs of the Pierres-Noires one foggy night in June 1896, on her return from South Africa. Out of the four hundred persons on board only three were saved. The following morning they were discovered by some fishermen from Ouessant, clinging on to a rock. Hundreds of bodies were recovered and buried at Molène. The British Government, in return for the services rendered, gave the islanders two things that were lacking on Molène—a cistern for storing water and a clock for the church tower. In the sacristy of the church you will be shown a richly jewelled chalice, also presented by the English in grateful memory of the kindness of the fisherfolk of Molène on this tragic occasion.

Molène is entirely without resources, except fish and rain-water. All provisions have to be brought from the mainland. Often in winter the inhabitants are several weeks without a boat being able to land supplies.

After a short call at Molène, the steamer proceeds to *Ouessant,* crossing the dangerous "Passage du Fromveur," dreaded by nervous passengers. Except in westerly gales, one generally lands at the little quay at *Lampaul,* close to the village of the same name, but in winter the force of the seas rolling in from the Atlantic makes it necessary for the steamer to put in to *Porz-Arland* or the Bay of Stiff, below the lighthouse on the north of the island.

The Isle of Ouessant (Enez Eussa in Breton) is the most remote and the highest of all the numerous islands off the coast of Brittany. It is ten miles from the mainland at the nearest point, eight kilometres long and three kilometres wide. On all sides it is surrounded by steep and broken granite cliffs that reach a height of fifty metres near the north end of the island. It would take too long to tell in detail the legendary history of Ouessant. It is mentioned by Pytheas of Marseilles as early as 400 B.C. Its remote and inaccessible situation at the end of the then known world gave it a certain notoriety. Some historians maintain that it was a stronghold of the worshippers of the Sun God. It is certain that it was long regarded as the last resting-place of the souls of the departed. Until they were destroyed and used in the construction of the first lighthouse, the island was scattered with dolmens, cromlechs, and other remains of Druidic and pre-Druidic worship. In the sixth century the Welsh monk, Saint Paul Aurelian, landed in the bay that still retains his name, Lan-Paul, or Porz-Paul, and built the first Christian church on Ouessant. In 1388 the English landed on the island and massacred the inhabitants. In 1778 the French fleet under Philippe Égalité defeated the English squadron commanded by Admiral Keppel within a few miles of the shore. Thirteen years later Chateaubriand, returning from America, was wrecked off Ouessant. Such are but a few important incidents in the maritime history of this remote island.

Practically all the male inhabitants out of a population of two thousand five hundred are seafarers. But comparatively little fishing is carried on, except in summer time in small open boats off-shore. In winter they are drawn up on to the cliffs, as it is generally too dangerous to venture out. And the fishermen have nothing to do but while away the long, dark days spending their earnings in the numerous cafés and *débits* which flourish in every quarter of the island. The majority of the menfolk of Ouessant are to be found in the *marine marchande* or in the *marine de guerre*. It is seldom they can manage to get home to see their wives and families; and wherever one goes on the island one is conscious of the overwhelming predominance of black-dressed women, with their hair flowing down to their waists.

"Qui voit Belle-Ile, voit son île; qui voit Groix, voit sa joie; qui voit Ouessant, voit son sang," runs the old Breton proverb. And it is well expressed, for even on the brightest day in midsummer, when the sun is shining and the sky and the sea are unruffled blue, there is always something sinister and mysterious about Ouessant. But when a damp fog is rolling in from the Atlantic and all is shrouded in a grey clammy mist; when the three sirens of Créach, Stiff, and La Jument are moaning piteously every few minutes to warn ships to keep far off this dangerous coast, then I know of no more terrifying spot in the whole world. These strange-looking rocks, standing up on the far end of the island beyond the chapel of Notre-Dame de Bon Voyage, take upon themselves the shape of petrified mastodons and other prehistoric monsters. The sea rolls in with its fury unchecked for more than four thousand miles of ocean, crashing against the rocks and sending showers of spray and spume for an amazing distance. The perpetual moaning of the trio of sirens

is answered back by the more distant tones of liners and tramp steamers of all nations which, in endless procession, are always passing up and down the Channel not so vary far off Ouessant, and which, on a fine day, afford a never-ceasing prospect of interest from its cliffs.

In sheltered coves on all sides of the island one comes across fishing-boats such as I have sketched in three of the illustrations to this book;[1] boats whose interest lies in their extraordinarily primitive construction and build. There

"PLATS" ON THE BEACH, PORZ-KINZY, OUESSANT

is no island off Europe quite like Ouessant, its only rival in Brittany being the minute Ile-de-Sein.

It is from Audierne that one embarks for the *Ile-de-Sein*; the passage, of uncertain duration, being generally made in the smack *Zénith* that acts as mail boat as well as carrying provisions and supplies for the island. One is never quite sure when she will start; it depends on wind, tide, cargo, and a hundred and one eventualities. The quay is crowded up with boxes, crates, meat, vegetables, wine barrels, furniture—sooner or later they are all stowed away in the hold—the mail-bags are fetched from the post office, the passengers, if there are any, get on board, the ropes are

[1] pp. 3, 141, 144.

cast off, the motor starts and one gets under way. We steer our course carefully through sardine boats, pass out over the bar at the harbour mouth, and very soon begin to feel the motion of the great long rollers of the Atlantic.

The coastline stretches away to the westward—an unbroken line of cliffs surmounted by a bare windswept-looking countryside, broken here and there by the spires of village churches: Saint-Tugen, Saint-Yves, Saint-They, Goulien, Primelin, Plogoff, — to mention but a few. Sardine boats are fishing a mile or so to the south: in the far distance to the south-west, if it is clear, one distinguishes the lighthouse of Eckmühl.

There is a long, undulating swell: the *Zénith* rolls and pitches, the passengers become more and more silent; presently one of them leans over the bulwarks and is sea-sick! Others soon follow the example. The skipper and mate converse in Breton. For an hour or more we sail on, tacking from time to time according to the direction of the wind. Eventually we are abreast of a solitary church standing on the cliffs. It is the famous shrine of Notre-Dame de Bon Voyage—*Itron Varia ar Veac'h Mad*, as she is called in Breton. If there are any "Iliens," i.e. women from the Ile-de-Sein, on board, they rouse themselves and piously make the sign of the cross. Perhaps it is now nearing midday. "L'Angélus, s'il vous plaît, messieurs," announces the skipper who is at the helm. And turning in the direction of the chapel on the cliffs we make the responses while he recites the well-known prayers said by Catholics all the world over three times daily, in memory of the Incarnation of the Son of God. But in Brittany one never forgets the souls of the departed, especially those who have been lost at sea; so the skipper starts the Psalm *De Profundis*, which every one seems to know by heart. . . . *Requiem æternam dona eis Domine*, he prays, and our *Requiescant in pace* mingles with the whistling of the wind in the rigging and the murmur of the waves.

Before long we have passed the Pointe du Raz, and our course lies across the dreaded "Raz," when the wind and tide meet, and where it is dangerous to venture here in any small craft. It would be difficult to say how many lives have been lost in this channel.

Doue va sikourit, evit tremen ar Raz;
Rag ma vag zo bihan hag ar mor a zo braz!

"Save me, O Lord, from the channel of the Raz, for my bark is so small and the sea is so great," says the old Breton prayer. And one never realizes its significance until one actually finds oneself in a small boat in the midst of these swirling masses of water.

To the north lies the lighthouse of *La Vieille*, rising up out of the sea on its isolated rock; two miles farther west is *Tévennec*—another rocky islet with a powerful lighthouse. Many other evil-looking rocks begin to appear: Les Baullets, Basse-Moudron, Basse-Triton. Ahead of us appears to be a cluster of houses apparently rising out of the water, beyond which is a tall lighthouse. That is one's first impression of the Ile-de-Sein as one approaches it by sea. At last the skipper steers the *Zénith* into the sheltered bay that forms a natural harbour for the large fleet of fishing-boats belonging to the island, and presently one is stepping ashore on the slippery landing-place, under the curious but respectful gaze of what seems to be the entire population, for whom the bi-weekly arrival of the *Zénith* in fine weather is the chief excitement of their lives.

The Ile-de-Sein is no more than two kilometres long, and less than one kilometre at its greatest width. In reality it is nothing more than the exposed portion of a reef of rocks just a few yards above high-water mark. But it is one of the most interesting spots in Europe, where, owing to its isolation and difficulty of access, the inhabitants have so far managed to remain almost untouched by the advance of modern civilization. How long they will remain so is doubtful.

The legendary history of the island goes back to remote antiquity. In Druidic times, it was supposed to have been the home of the nine sacred Virgins, who were consulted as oracles by the few who ever ventured to penetrate out to this sea-girt sanctuary. The Ile-de-Sein disputes with Ouessant the honour of being the place where the Druids were buried. The inhabitants on the mainland certainly regarded it as the Ultima Thule, where the souls of the departed were taken by sea at night to repose in peace. Indeed the island was looked upon with such fear and dread that few persons ever dared to land on its rocky shore. It was given a wide berth. In this way an incredible amount of superstitious beliefs grew up connected with the mysterious *Enez-Sizun*, or *Insula Sena* (as it is called by the ancient geographers). But sailors knew that there was no better place for fishing anywhere off the coast than this still uninhabited reef of rocks. And one day some of them so far ventured as to land there, built a few rude huts out of stones and wreckage; eventually removed themselves and their families from the mainland. Half savage, still almost pagan, the first inhabitants of the Ile-de-Sein managed to exist on the products of the fishing and on the spoils of wrecks. By the beginning of the seventeenth century the *Iliens* had an unenviable and sinister reputation as professional wreckers. Many a ship went ashore on the island, lured to destruction by the lights exposed by the natives. A Jesuit priest, Père Michel le Nobletz, whom we have already mentioned in our description of the port of Le Conquet, and who had given up his life to the conversion of the inhabitants of these islands lying off the coast of Finistère, landed here one day. He preached with such earnestness that it was not long before he had won the hearts of these simple people. He taught them the Catholic religion, baptized them, and before leaving the island, instructed an old sailor, François Le Luc, who knew how to read, to gather them together on Sundays, so that they might recite the Litanies of the Saints, and follow the prayers of the Mass, even if they had no priest to offer the Holy Sacrifice of the Altar. Not content with this, Père le Nobletz sent his sailor catechist a book of sermons, and on Good Friday the old fisherman preached the Passion to his fellow seafarers and their families.

For many years, despite repeated petitions to the Bishop of Quimper, no priest could be found for the island. Finally Le Luc went to the bishop and asked if he himself might be ordained. The bishop agreed, and this elderly fisherman was sent off to the Benedictines at Landévennec, where he did his studies, being afterwards ordained at Saint-Pol-de-Léon. He then returned to the Ile-de-Sein, where for seven years he lived the life of a model *curé*. He taught the fishermen *cantiques* which they used to sing at sea: "Cette musique si agréable aux Anges, semble avoir adouci la terreur des Flots, de sorte que depuis, les naufrages sont beaucoup plus rares," naively remarks a contemporary author.

After the death of Le Luc the islanders were left without a resident priest for many years. Indeed it was not until well on into the nineteenth century that we find a regular succession of *curés*. Most priests were unable to stand the loneliness and isolation of this often inaccessible island. At the time of the Revolution there were

ILE-DE-SEIN

350 persons on the Ile-de-Sein; the present population numbers about 1050.

The village is grouped around the church at the extreme east end of the island. There are no streets properly so-called, the houses being huddled together as close as possible and divided by narrow alleys, not much more than a yard wide, reminding one of the "rows" in Great Yarmouth, or "calle" in Venice. The reason of this curious arrangement is mainly due to the extreme value of every inch of land on the island. For a similar reason the fields, if one may describe the tiny little stone-walled patches of sandy soil as fields, are seldom more than two or three square yards in area. A few cows somehow manage to find enough to eat on the scrubby grass and weeds. There are no other animals save dogs and cats. Horses are unknown. More than once within a hundred years, during an exceptionally high tide, the sea has washed right over the island, the inhabitants being obliged to take refuge in the upper stories of their strongly built, thick-walled houses. Once they were left seventeen days without communication with the mainland, and nearly died of starvation. And it was over three years before it was possible to raise any more crops, so impregnated with salt was the sandy soil.

Owing to the continual intermarriage which has been going on for so long, the unity and characteristic features of this hardy race of seafarers have been wonderfully preserved. What a splendid type they are, both the men and the women! The former seem to possess something of the primitive simplicity that one only finds among savage races, and yet what gracious and winning hospitality they bestow on a stranger in their midst. On the Ile-de-Sein one is never conscious of that strange antagonism that confronts one in so many fishing villages on the mainland of Brittany.

All the women, old and young, are uniformly dressed in sombre black. Somehow one has the feeling that one has strayed into the enclosure of a convent of nuns when one beholds these dark-eyed, dark-haired women going about their work, robed in black, with black veils over their heads. There are said to be only twenty-seven surnames among the inhabitants and almost every one is related to every one else!

Marriage ceremonies are far less elaborate than those on the mainland. The prospective bride and bridegroom each give a banquet in their houses to their own immediate relatives, the guests contributing their share of the repast. The following morning the bridal couple go to Holy Communion at Mass, and in the evening there is another festal meal, followed by a dance. Next morning Mass is said in church for departed relations, and afterwards the bride and bridegroom visit the churchyard to pray for the souls of those nearest of kin. For a whole month the newly-wedded bride abstains from work in the fields. Women on the Ile-de-Sein do not "tutoyer" their husbands, nor yet their sons (i.e. use the familiar second person singular as is almost universal elsewhere). Women address each other as *va c'hoar* (my sister), and the men call each other *va breur* (my brother).

All the work on the land is done by women. When on shore the men occupy the time in mending their nets, repairing their lobster-pots and boats. The woman is the householder: she gathers seaweed, makes iodine, tills the soil, grows corn. There is no public register of land. Division of landed property takes place on the day of a funeral: the actual division of the fields being decided by a curious ceremony of a child throwing pebbles which have been put in his cap by all the women present. The bit of ground on which a particular pebble falls becomes the property of the woman or her representative, who put it in the child's cap. The men are often ignorant of the exact locality of the land owned by their family!

Nowhere else in France, and in few places in Europe, has the old clan or tribe system survived so completely as among the fisherfolk of the Ile-de-Sein. It would be hard to discover a more devout or religious people. Religion is the absorbing interest of their lives. Every morning at Mass the church is crowded with men and women. Many communicate daily. On Sundays you find yourself surrounded by fishermen, old and young, who follow the Mass word for word in their large and well-thumbed prayer-books, joining in the singing with voices that sound like the roar of the ocean. Never have I worshipped in such a homely, earnest, and intelligent congregation. Missions, retreats, devotions for the special seasons of the year, here provide the intellectual and emotional outlet that in most other fishing villages on the mainland is now supplied by the cinema. Not content with this, both men and women are constantly undertaking pilgrimages to favourite sanctuaries, such as Sainte-Anne-d'Auray. Many of them have been to Lourdes and even Rome. Vocations to the priesthood and the religious life are frequent among this race of seafarers.

A cheery, bright, and hospitable people—yet always haunted by the presence of Death. The next world is a tremendous reality, almost as concrete and tangible to the average "Ilien" as the material

WRECKED STEAMER, ILE-DE-SEIN

universe which surrounds him. The air is full of the presence of
the departed: they rise out of the sea; they are visible among the
rocks and on the shore; they are heard whispering behind the stone
walls that divide the fields. Once a year, at night time, he will see
the mysterious ship of the dead, the *bag-noz*, sailing past the island,
blazing with light, and commanded by the sailor who died first
within the previous twelve months. After dark he will be careful
not to bang a door, for it may give pain, or disturb the repose of
some wandering soul. "Joa d'ann anaoun" (Joy to the holy
souls) is a favourite greeting, to which one replies "Amen."

The cemetery is so small that only a few permanent graves are
allowed; after a certain time the bones are dug up and placed in
an ossuary.

On the death of a fisherman, his family offer a banquet to all
his near relations and friends. One of the guests pronounces an
oration concerning the departed man, then prayers are said for
the repose of his soul. His children or orphans are always cared
for by relations. There is no form of public relief.

If a sailor dies away from the island, a cloth is laid on a table in
his house, upon which are placed two white napkins in the form of
a cross. A portrait of the dead man, or if this is lacking some
object that belonged to him, is laid in the centre, between two
candlesticks and the crucifix brought from the church. The choir
come in, sing the *Placebo*, and all night long a watch is kept up and
prayers said, just as is done if the corpse is present, and the usual
Requiem Masses are celebrated.

Indeed prayer for the dead is part and parcel of everyday life
on the Ile-de-Sein. Requiem Masses are said as often as the
Church allows, and almost every morning you will find a priest
and a little acolyte hurrying through one or more Offices for the
Dead, which pious persons have requested for the repose of some
relative. Another curious custom is a collection made all round the
village on the night of All Saints for money to pay Masses and
Offices to be said for the departed. The collection takes place at
night, four men repairing to the church to toll the bell while the
other four are begging alms. The latter, armed with a hand-bell,

stop at each house where a death has recently occurred, crying out: "Christenien, difunit, ha lavaromp eun *De Profundis* evit an anaon tremenet" (Christians awake! pray to God for the souls of the dead, and say for their intentions one *De Profundis*). Those within the house recite the psalm, the young men outside concluding with a lusty "Requiescant in pace."

The sailors of the island also preserve a curious belief in the material aspect of life after death. On some of the older tombs there are holes carved out for libations of milk and wine—at least so it is said, although nowadays they are filled with holy water.

Most of the families on the Ile-de-Sein are fairly prosperous, and live in solidly built, two-storied stone houses, many of which are whitewashed outside.

Practically all the provisions have to be brought from the mainland. Apart from fish, the only products of the island are barley, potatoes, rye, and aniseed. There are, so I understand, no less than twenty-seven *débits*, or public-houses, on this tiny island of little more than a thousand inhabitants. Drink, as everywhere else in Brittany, is the chief vice of the inhabitants. From time to time there will be a sort of epidemic of drunkenness, when the fishermen suddenly revert to the state of primitive savagery in which they existed previous to the eighteenth century. "*Alors ils sont comme de bêtes féroces*, like wild beasts," explained one of the local priests to me; "when they start drinking one can do nothing with them. And then, after a while, all is over and they become quiet again."

The islanders pay no taxes, a state of affairs unique in France.

The men sell their fish either locally or else land it, or dispatch it in boxes to Audierne or Douarnenez. Crayfish and turbot are the most valuable fish caught. Most of the local boats are small, undecked, cutter-rigged craft, with crews of three or four men, who are paid on a share basis. Fishing is carried on throughout the year, but chiefly in the spring and autumn. The boats are generally built either at Camaret or Roscoff.

In every skipper's house you find suspended from the ceiling a boat made from the hollowed-out crust of a loaf of brown bread, sloop-rigged, with paper sails. Once a year, the Sunday before

Lent, the skipper invites all his crew to supper. It is the *Fête du bateau*, or *Fest ar vag*. They sit down to a substantial meal of soup, fresh meat, and vegetables, followed by a cake made of wheat flour, prunes, and eggs. A litre of wine is set before each man. The crew provide brandy. At the end of the repast the men stand up, holding their caps in their hands. The boat is taken down from the ceiling by the oldest man present. Then the skipper makes the sign of the cross, and breaks the bread of which it is made, dividing the pieces among the crew. It is regarded as a sacramental rite, uniting them together, body and soul. One of the men then takes the new loaf on the table, hollows out the crust, and rigs up a boat like the old one just taken down. They salute it three times while reciting together the *Veni Creator*. Grace is then said and the ceremony is over. On the following Friday a *maigre* dinner of fish and potatoes is provided by the crew; the *mousse* afterwards distributing to widows or poor relations what may be left of the brandy.

One cannot leave the Ile-de-Sein without mentioning wrecks, for they are an inseparable part of the island life. (You will see a recent wreck in the drawing on page 151). At one time wrecks were the chief source of income to the inhabitants: their houses were furnished with the fittings of ships; they provisioned themselves with ships' stores. But nowadays this is but a memory of the past, and whenever a ship runs aground on this rocky shore, the "Iliens" are the first to try to save those on board, the lifeboat venturing out in all but the worst storms. A touching record of the kindness shown by the islanders to the crew of an English cargo-boat may be seen in a large oil-painting hanging up in the church, representing Our Lady, Star of the Sea, presented by the British Government as a token of their appreciation of the unselfish behaviour towards the survivors.

I make no apologies for having devoted such an undue amount of space to this tiny island, little more than a mile long. For here, as nowhere else on the mainland, does one come into contact with the mariner of Brittany at his best. Here he is unspoilt, almost untouched by the brutalizing influences of a civilization to which he seems unable to adapt himself without being ruined, morally and socially. His childlike character belongs to a bygone age; his virtues are the product of a Christian society that is rapidly passing away. Here on this little island, so small and so low that it might at any moment be washed away in some storm of unusual violence, you find the last refuge of what was best in a once Catholic Europe, and which sooner or later may have disappeared altogether.[1]

[1] For much of the information in this chapter I am indebted to Monsieur Charles Le Goffic's *Sur la Côte* (Paris, 1928).

CHAPTER XIII

THE great, landlocked harbour of *Brest* has much in common with Milford Haven, in South Wales. There is the same kind of scenery on the shores of both; the same climatic and atmospheric conditions prevail; but the Rade de Brest is of much greater extent than the now almost deserted anchorage in Pembrokeshire; its strategic importance to France far greater than that of Milford Haven is to Britain.

On approaching Brest from the Chenal du Four one sails eastwards for about five miles after leaving Pointe Saint-Mathieu with the coastline on either side. Having arrived at the lighthouse on the Pointe de Minou one enters the one-and-a-half-mile-wide channel known as Le Goulet, which forms a sort of bottleneck entrance to the famous *rade* that opens out some three miles farther on and which forms one of the most capacious natural harbours in Europe. Artificial breakwaters have been constructed on the west, south, and east of the immediate area facing the town of Brest, affording additional protection in rough weather for the ships of the *marine de guerre* as well as those of the *marine marchande* always to be found here.

The older part of the *arsenal*, or dockyard, of Brest is situated in a narrow winding valley through which flows the River Penfeld. There is very little space on either side of the stream, which is now walled in so as to form a wet dock. In this confined area are graving docks, workshops, victualling yard, and naval hospital. The *arsenal* has been extended in recent years at Laninon, on the west side of the Penfeld, on the low-lying land in front of the *rade-abri*, with two large fitting basins, two dry docks, oil tanks, and harbour for torpedo boats. In the *rade* there are always anchored a number of warships, including the two obsolete battleships, *Armorique* and *Magellan*, occupied by the Ecole des Mousses, or boys' training establishment. The naval cadets, or *aspirants*, formerly quartered in the old three-decker *Borda*, have now been removed to barracks overlooking the port of Laninon.

The maritime history of Brest dates from the times of the Romans,

BREST: PORT DE COMMERCE

who had a military post, Gesocribate, where now stands the château. In 875 the town was attacked by Saxon pirates, who were eventually repulsed. Edward III of England sailed up to Brest with his ships in 1342, besieged and captured Brest, which did not surrender to the French until 1397. During the Wars of the League the port was frequently attacked by the English and Spanish. In 1513 took place the famous fight between the *Belle-Cordelière* and the English fleet. The present prosperity of Brest dates from 1631, when Richelieu began the construction of the dockyard. It was added to by Colbert and Duquesne. The ramparts were put up according to the plans of Vauban, after he had repulsed an assault of nearly a hundred British and Dutch vessels. During the eighteenth century the fortifications of Brest were strengthened and added to; the Naval Hospital and the Church of Saint-Louis, full of memorials to bygone sailors, were built. The last occasion when the port was subjected to an attack by the English fleet took place in 1794, when the French squadron of twenty-six sail of the line and seven frigates, under Villaret-Joyeuse, was defeated on the "glorious First of June" by the English squadron commanded by Admiral Howe, a battle famous for the heroic resistance of the *Vengeur*.

Brest is a typical dockyard town. Its very existence seems to depend on the navy in much the same way as does that of Portsmouth or Devonport, perhaps even more so. The streets are always full of naval officers and bluejackets, and no matter where one goes, one is conscious of the presence of the *marine de guerre* somewhere in the background.

But within recent years it has developed considerably as a commercial port, a new harbour having been built below the ramparts, where two long jetties protected by a mole afford a safe anchorage. Between the jetties are three other projecting quays. Vegetables are exported in large quantities, while coal, timber, and wine are perhaps the chief imports. Fishing-boats from various ports in Finistère land much of their catch here, and the *port de commerce* at Brest is now almost the busiest commercial port in Brittany with the exception of Nantes and Saint-Malo.

During the war Brest was one of the chief bases where American troops were landed, and American financiers and business-men had dreams that if only the navy would transfer its arsenal and dockyard west of the mouth of the Penfeld, a vast up-to-date modern commercial port, superior to any other in France, might be created here, so that Brest would become the chief continental port for

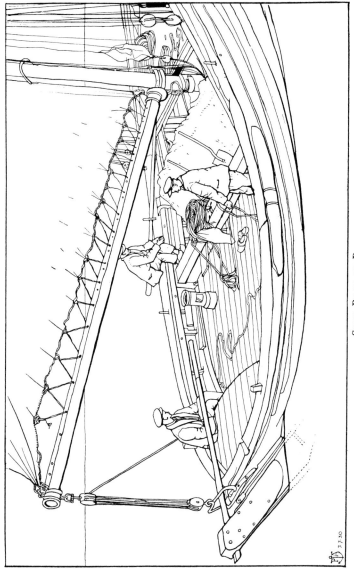

SAND BOAT AT BREST

transatlantic liners.   But this scheme has not materialized and
Brest goes on in the same way as before.

When wandering about the streets of Brest you cannot help recalling Pierre Loti's numerous references to the old grey town in
his Breton novels.   For instance there is his description of a typical
winter's evening at Brest in *Mon Frère Yves*.[1]   You feel the fine
drizzling rain that falls continuously, making the steep slate roofs
of the tall granite houses look blacker than usual.   It falls on the
noisy, hustling crowd of a Sunday evening, jostling each other in
the narrow streets under a sky of unbroken greyness.

"Drunken sailors are singing, soldiers stumble, making a clinking
sound with their swords, the rest of the crowd wander about aim-
lessly—workmen with drawn and haggard expressions; women in
their little woollen shawls and pointed *coiffes* of muslin walk past,
their rosy faces lit up and smelling of brandy; drunken old men and
women who have fallen down and who have been picked up, and
whose backs are covered with mud.

"The rain falls and goes on falling.   Everything is wet; the old-
fashioned, buckled hats of the Bretons, the sailors' caps stuck on
the side of their heads, the beribboned shakos, the white coifs, and
the umbrellas.

"The whole atmosphere is so black, so gloomy, that it is difficult
to realize that the sun exists.   One feels imprisoned beneath layers
of heavy damp clouds that soak one.   It seems that they could
never come to an end, and that behind them is the sky.   One
breathes water.

"The sailors with their singing impart to the streets a strange
note of youth and gaiety; their wide, pale-blue collars and red
pom-poms in contrast to the dark blue of the rest of their uniforms.
They wander from one cabaret to another, pushing every one aside,
making nonsensical remarks, but which seem to amuse themselves.
They stop beneath a porch, or in front of the shops where are
exposed articles for their use: red handkerchiefs, in the midst of
which are displayed wonderful ships—*La Bretagne, La Triomphante,*
or *La Dévastation*[2]; ribbons for their caps with the names worked in

[1] c. iii.   [2] Seldom seen nowadays.

gold; little objects made of rope for making fast those canvas sacks in which on board they keep their belongings; elegant *amarrages* in sennit, i.e. plaited rope yarn, for a *gabier*[1] to hang his big knife round his neck; silver whistles for *quartier-maîtres*, red belts, little combs and mirrors.

"From time to time a gust of wind blows off their caps, and makes the drunkards reel. And then the rain falls heavier than before, beating down like torrents of hail.

"The crowd of sailors grows thicker. One sees them surging in masses along the entrance to the rue de Siam. They come up from the dockyard and the *ville basse* by the steep granite steps, scattering themselves over the streets, singing all the while.

"Those who have come in from the *rade* are wetter than the others. They have been drenched with salt water, as well as soaked with rain. Their sail-boats heel over under a biting squall and rise to meet the sea which covers them with spume, bearing them rapidly into harbour. The men climb the steps with eagerness, shaking themselves like half-drowned cats.

"The wind swirls down the long streets, forecasting a stormy night."

And Loti goes on to describe the crowds of women who under umbrellas and mackintoshes are waiting at the top of the steps above the dockyard for their menfolk to come ashore: old women and young girls—mothers, wives, and sweethearts. He pictures them in a few minutes, arm in arm, walking up the old dark streets of Recouvrance, with their tall houses of granite, climbing the steep stairs to a damp room which smells of drains and the mouldiness of poverty, where amid a layer of dust are displayed shells and bottles mixed up with curios from foreign parts. And thanks to the brandy, rum, or wine bought at the cabaret down below, they will be able to forget that cruel separation of many months or years.[2]

But there are other sailors that go off in another direction— towards the infamous rue des Sept-Saints, where women are already on the watch for them: standing in their doorways or beckoning

[1] In the days of sail a "topman." [2] Chap. iv.

from their windows: women with drink-sodden voices and horrible gestures.

Before very long they will have earned their ill-gotten gains. Sailors the first day they come ashore are generous. In addition to what they give themselves, there is always that which can be taken from them, when, if one is lucky, they happen to be blind drunk.

The men look about them undecided, as if they are scared, simply because they find themselves on land once more.

Where shall we go? Where shall we start? . . .

The wind, the cold winter rain, and the darkness of the night— all these add to the pleasure for those who have a home to go to. But for the rest—those who do not belong to Brest—it is a different matter. So they start off, walking arm in arm, laughing at every- thing, wandering first to the right, then to the left, like wild beasts that have just been let out of captivity.

And then Loti makes Yves and his shipmates turn into the little cabaret "*A la Descente des Navires,* chez Madame Creachcadec," a *bouge* in the rue de Siam.

"Within the warm atmosphere reeks of drink. There is a charcoal fire in a brazier . . . at the back of the cabaret the dinner is cooking on the stove, throwing out a smell of good soup.

"In the streets is the sound of an uproar. A group of sailors arrive, singing at the top of their voices to a lively tune, these words remembered from the Liturgy of the Church: '*Kyrie Christe, Domi- num nostrum, Kyrie eleison.* . . .'

"They enter, knocking over the chairs, and at the same time a gust of west wind puts out the lamps.

"*Kyrie Christe, Dominum nostrum.* . . . Bretons do not like this sort of humour, which comes no doubt from the lower quarters of some big industrial city. Nevertheless the contrast between the words and the music is funny, and that makes them laugh. . . .

"It is terribly stuffy in the cabaret, the din uproarious. Madame Creachcadec brings in hot wine all steaming—first service of dinner ordered—heads begin to turn!

"In the rue des Sept-Saints and in the rue Saint-Yves the sound of singing and harsh cries goes on till morning. It is as if the barbarians, the hordes of ancient Gaul, have been let loose: scenes that recall the orgies of primitive savages.

"The sailors go on singing. The women—excited and dishevelled—wait for the moment when they can seize their money, their harsh voices mingling with the deeper tones of the men.

"They sing, these sailors, at the top of their voices, but with a sort of childlike innocence, words of an unblushing coarseness, or else folk-songs of the Midi, Basque airs—but above all those plaintive Breton compositions, that seem to be tunes of the *biniou* handed down from remote antiquity.

". . . The night wears on: the brothels alone remain open, and in the streets the rain falls mercilessly upon an exuberance of savage debauchery."[1]

Do not imagine that this is a photograph of twentieth-century Brest. Times and manners have changed since Loti wrote his famous novel. The Brest he is describing is the Brest of 1870. And Brest in 1930 is as different from Brest fifty years ago as is the Portsmouth of to-day from that naval base at the same epoch. Yet despite all the changes that have taken place, despite all the superficial improvements in social customs, the greater refinement and luxury of the present generation, the soul of the sailor, particularly the Breton sailor, has not altered so very greatly. I have often watched similar scenes to those described in *Mon Frère Yves* when looking down on to the dockyard from the top of the steps beside the Pont-Transbordeur when "liberty men" are coming ashore. I have mixed with them in the crowded streets of this grey-granite town when the rain fell as pitilessly as Loti has described it. I have mingled with this crowd of cherry-red pom-pomed *col-bleus* striding along arm in arm and singing at the top of their voices as they rolled down the rue de Siam. "*A la Descente des Navires*, chez Madame Creachcadec" may have disappeared in the course of rebuilding. "Cette Madame Creachcadec, une vraie mère pour tous les matelots," who knew all her *clientèle* by name, has gone to her reward long ago, but other "Mesdames

[1] Chap. iv.

Creachcadec" have taken her place, and in many a little cabaret and *débit* at the foot of the rue de Siam or in the neighbourhood, you can still find such scenes of revelry if you look for them, possibly a shade more decorous; or outside the town at the lower end of the rue Jean-Jaurès, near the merry-go-rounds and the booths on the place de la Liberté, in summer time.

Nowadays there will generally be a jazz band or a mechanical piano to accompany the singing; increased vigilance on the part of the police make it necessary to observe certain conventions in public, but the sailor is still the same, and those who can earn a living in catering for his pleasure when he is ashore know what he is after, and are waiting to satisfy his demands so long as he has the money to pay.

Here in Brest, as in Saint-Malo and other Breton ports, you may still discover, not unfrequently if you happen to be up and about unusually early or unusually late, "a dark mass having the shape of a human being lying in the gutter," [1] in one of those deserted streets beneath the overhanging ramparts. A sailor, who in trying to get back to his ship has fallen down in a drunken stupor and remained there, unable to pick himself up again. Sometimes he is removed by the gendarmes, at other times a shipmate or a woman drags him off.

The Brest that Loti depicted is still there, under the surface—a fascinating Brest of a strangely attractive personality, despite its grey skies, grey granite, and frequent rain! The charm and interest of Brest lies in the fact that within its walls one can study the Breton sailor drawn from all parts of his country. During the evenings the streets are crowded with them. The whole maritime world of Brittany seems concentrated in this old grey town. If it is summer, you can watch these mariners of Brittany amusing themselves among the booths, swings, and merry-go-rounds on the place de la Liberté; you can sit among them and listen to their conversation in the cafés. If you have the *entrée* you can study them, particularly the young *mousses*, in either the Foyer du Marin beyond the ramparts, or in the Cercle Catholique du Marin et du

---

[1] *Mon Frère Yves*, chap. v.

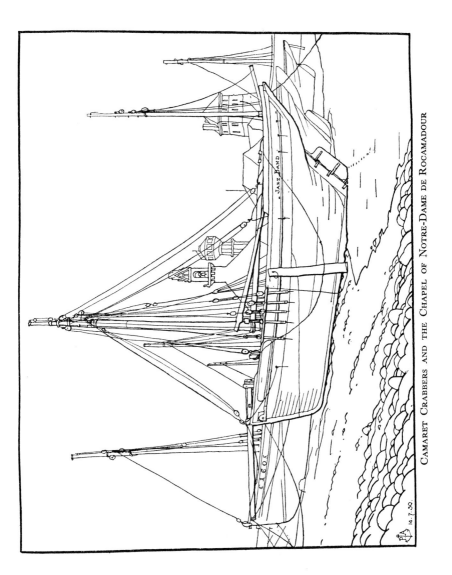

CAMARET CRABBERS AND THE CHAPEL OF NOTRE-DAME DE ROCAMADOUR

Soldat in the rue d'Aiguillon. You can take one of the pleasure steamers that make trips on Sundays to one of the various places on the *rade*, and there are sure to be a swarm of *col-bleus* among the passengers, laughing, joking, and singing with all the high spirits of youth.

Brest is a much-maligned town. It does not always rain here. And when the sun is shining and great masses of cumulus cloud are drifting across the sky and making dark shadows on the blue waters of the *rade*, there are few more attractive places anywhere in France than this great naval base, the heart of maritime Brittany.

There are quite a number of small ports situated on the Rade de Brest or farther inland on the estuaries of the various rivers which flow into it.

Landerneau lies eleven miles up the River Élorn, and is only accessible at high water. It does a certain amount of trade, pit-props being exported; timber, coal, and chemical manures are unloaded at the quays which extend for a short distance on either side of the river. A small quay used by coasting vessels is also to be found at *Daoulas*, three or four miles up the river of the same name. Cargo-boats are often found anchored off *Landévennec*, while *Port-Launay*, thirteen miles beyond, is quite a busy little place for the export and import of agricultural produce.

Le Fret, Quélern, and *Roscanvel* are three villages on the western shores of the *rade*, the first-named sheltering a few fishing-boats and coasting vessels, and the place where Jeanne de Navarre, Duchess of Brittany, embarked in 1403 to marry Henry IV of England.

Camaret, eight kilometres west of Le Fret, situated on a bay facing the open sea, but well protected from the ocean, is one of the most interesting and important fishing centres in Finistère, with a character quite different to either Concarneau, Douarnenez, or Audierne. Its history goes back to a remote antiquity. It seems to have been a centre of Druidic worship. In the fourth century a Welsh hermit, Saint Rick, settled here. During the Middle Ages Camaret was constantly attacked by pirates, later on by the English, Dutch, and Spanish. In 1594 the latter built the fort at Roscanvel on what is still known as the Pointe des Espagnols. But the event in their history of which the inhabitants prefer to remember is the Anglo-Dutch defeat in 1694 off the shore of Tierz-Roux; a Dutch frigate being left stranded on Camaret spit and an English transport with five hundred men on board being sunk at the bottom of the Iroise. A souvenir of this naval engagement still remains, for a cannon-ball carried off the top of the spire of the chapel of Notre-Dame de Rocamadour. This curious old church was built in 1560 and dedicated in memory of the shrine at Rocamadour in the *département* of Lot, a great place of pilgrimage with sailors. Close to the church is a fort erected by Vauban in 1689. Within a few miles of the shore was fought in 1759 the famous engagement between *La Belle Poule* and the "saucy *Arethusa*." It was off Camaret that Fulton demonstrated before Napoleon his submarine, the *Nautile*, in 1801. He attacked a British seventy-two-gun ship lying in the bay, but she got away before the submarine could approach. Camaret to-day derives its prosperity from the fishing industry, and is famous for its lobsters, crabs, and crayfish (*langoustes*). Until two or three years ago the Camaret boats always fished off the Scilly Isles and Land's End, and were a familiar sight at Newlyn. But lately they have been going much more to the north coast of Africa. Sardines are also landed here, Camaret being the most northerly sardine port in Finistère. With its long quays, quaint streets, old boatbuilders' yards, and general atmosphere of busy prosperity, Camaret is a place in which one gladly lingers. In the summer time one can eat one's *déjeuner* or *dîner*, or sip one's *apéritif* outside the hotels or cafés, and watch the fishermen landing their catch a few yards away across the quay. In the two sketches of Camaret included in this book you will see the sort of fishing craft still found here, details of which I have given in another chapter.

On the south side of the Presqu'île de Crozon, at whose far end Camaret is situated, is the smaller port of *Morgat*, overlooking the Baie de Douarnenez. The inhabitants are mostly engaged in the sardine fisheries. The actual port is formed of a mole and a stone quay extending westward from the inner side of the mole. About seven miles across the bay in a south-easterly direction from Morgat lies the famous sardine port of Douarnenez.

Douarnenez with its thirteen thousand inhabitants is the chief sardine port in France: a busy, prosperous place, a curious mixture of a modern industrial town with a picturesque medieval fishing village, where the old and the new are always in antagonism and where, as nowhere else, one is fully conscious of the violent extremes of the Breton character.

Its origins are uncertain. It is possible that a Gallo-Roman settlement existed here. In the sixteenth century Douarnenez was an important seaport, often attacked, often pillaged. In 1595 the town was destroyed, the stones of the houses being used by the robber chief, Fontenelle, to fortify the Ile Tristran, which lies off the shore, where he established himself for three years, despite all efforts to force him to surrender.

Tortuous cobbled streets and alleys, with granite houses on either side, lead down to the harbour, which lies in a small bay completely sheltered from the prevailing westerly winds. Additional protection is afforded by a long stone jetty from which there is a magnificent view across the bay and where one can watch the entry and departure of the fishing fleet. During the summer months the narrow quays are the favourite haunt of artists, almost as numerous here as at Concarneau. The groupings of yellow, pink, green, and white tunny boats reflected in the blue water; the filmy, gauze-like blue sardine nets; the red, pink, and orange clothing of the fishermen; the shimmering of the little silver fish being brought ashore in baskets; the background of green wooded slopes or the architectural masses of the grey granite or whitewashed houses with their slate roofs, exercise a never-ending fascination for these painters, good, bad, and indifferent. They attack the scene in all conditions of light and atmosphere. You see them planting their easels at points of vantage early in the morning. They are here again when the sun goes down and the moon rises over the bay. The fishermen are so accustomed to their presence that they are seldom disturbed.

Such is the impression one gets of Douarnenez in summer; a place of sunshine and shadow. In winter the little narrow streets are damp and slippery, and more often than not it is raining. The only note of cheerfulness is to be found in the innumerable cafés, *estaminets*, and *débits*, with their ever-open doors inviting the fishermen to enter, and where he can escape the gloom of the Breton climate and drown his "Celtic melancholy" in drink.

The Douarnenez fisherman is proud of his port, and rightly so, for it has risen to its present importance almost entirely through his own initiative and hard work. Possibly he is the most intelligent and "go-ahead" of any Breton fisherman. He is less conservative in his outlook, always more ready to adopt new methods and to keep abreast with the times. He has all the weakness as well as the strength of his race. He is proud and independent: in these days almost invariably a rabid Socialist or Communist of a type unknown to us in this country. He despises the peasant and hates the middle-class *bourgeois*, the latter typified in his eyes by the fish-curer, with whom he is always in antagonism, and by whom he always imagines he is being exploited.

The Douarnenez fisherman is literally an *enfant terrible*: a child in his limited mental outlook, terrible in his fierce capacity for hatred and weakness for nursing a grievance. The natural charm of his racial temperament has, more often than not, been soured and embittered by harsh conflict with a lifelong fight against increasingly difficult industrial conditions and the monotonous grinding toil of his labour. Can it be wondered that he turns to militant socialism and looks towards Soviet Russia as the only remedy for the problems of life? He has lost his one-time childlike faith in the teachings of the Catholic Church. Nowadays he despises the priests as much as he despises the peasants of the country-side. He reads his revolutionary newspapers and listens to orators who preach communism to him, and for the moment puts the same trust in them as he once did in the sermons his grandfathers heard from their pulpit. One day perhaps he will be disillusioned. And what is going to happen then? One cannot say; but the Breton always swings from one extreme to the other. That alone is certain!

In addition to its fisheries Douarnenez carries on a certain amount of trade. In the *port de commerce*, situated on the west side of the town, and known as *Port-Rhu*, timber and coal are landed, and pit-props as well as other produce exported.

Opposite Douarnenez, at the mouth of the estuary upon which Port-Rhu lies, stands *Tréboul*, a picturesque fishing village of white-washed houses embowered in trees, also a fairly busy sardine port.

After leaving Tréboul there are no other ports on the south shore of the bay of Douarnenez. The rocky coast continues without a break as far as the Pointe du Van, beyond which lies the Baie des Trépassés, where, according to the old legends, the bodies of the Druids used to be taken by sea to be buried on the Ile-de-Sein. The place is also said to be the site of the Ville d'Ys, which was destroyed by the sea in the fifth century, and around whose mysterious end such strange stories have been woven.

The neighbouring villages of *Cléden-Cap-Sizun*, *Plogoff*, and *Primelin* are mostly inhabited by seafarers who in these days fish from Audierne, or who are serving in the mercantile marine. Between Primelin and Plogoff, in a prominent position on the cliffs, stands the pilgrimage shrine of Notre-Dame de Bon Voyage, whose Pardon on the second Sunday in July is attended by thousands of seamen and fishermen from all the surrounding district.

The *Pointe du Raz* enjoys a reputation in France similar to the Land's End in England; it is the real "Finis-terre" of Brittany, and the view from its cliffs, 230 ft. high, is quite enough to account for the presence here of a large hotel for the accommodation and refreshment of the tourists who flock here in motors and charabancs during the summer. Indeed, no tour in Brittany can be said to be complete without having "done" the Pointe du Raz. Close to the signal station stands a white marble statue of Notre-Dame des Naufragés, and on a small, isolated rock about three-quarters of a mile from the shore is the lighthouse of La Vieille.

At the Pointe du Raz the coastline continues in a south-easterly direction for about twenty kilometres, until after passing the Pointe de Lervily one is in sight of the houses and jetty of Audierne.

Audierne is one of the busiest sardine ports on the coast of Finistère. It is situated about three-quarters of a mile from the entrance of the harbour on the west side of the estuary of the River Goyen. It

FIND LAIR

AUDIERNE

is sheltered in all winds, and if it were not for the difficult and dangerous entrance, owing to a sand-bar over which the seas break, just beyond the end of the jetty, would be an ideal port. There are long quays facing the town. Both in Audierne itself and at *Poulgoazec,* on the opposite shore, there are numerous sardine factories, employing hundreds of women and girls. The harbour is almost dry at low water. Lobster fishing is also carried on here and mackerel are caught in the winter.

There is not much to relate concerning the maritime history of this busy sardine port. It is said to have been almost destroyed by the tidal wave that did so much harm at Penmarch in the sixteenth century. The streets are full of ancient houses, and in the porch of the old church, no longer used, are some curious carvings of ships over the doorway.

With its whitewashed buildings in startling contrast to the vivid green of the trees, the red trousers and jumpers of the fishermen, and the blue nets of the "sardiniers," Audierne is not far behind Concarneau and Douarnenez as a rival in picturesque charm, and every year attracts not a few artists. One of my drawings gives an impression of the harbour as seen from Poulgoazec, the other shows a view of the quays against which are moored the sardine boats.

At high water small cargo-boats sometimes proceed up the river to *Pont-Croix,* five kilometres from Audierne, where there is a short quay.

There are no other ports between Audierne and Saint-Guénolé just north of the Pointe de Penmarch, a distance of about twenty kilometres. The bay is exposed to all the winds between south and north-west and affords no shelter. In stormy weather the breakers extend over a mile from the shore.

CHAPTER XIV

THE country around Penmarch is unique in France. The coast is low and barren, surrounded by dangerous reefs of underlying rocks. For centuries this was one of the most prosperous parts of Brittany. Through two ports, Saint-Guénolé and Kérity, commercial relations were maintained with various countries, especially Spain and the Mediterranean. *Penmarch* at one time owned more trading vessels than Nantes. The surrounding district seems to have been more fertile than to-day. Cod and hake could be caught in large quantities within a comparatively short distance of the shore. There was a sheltered harbour that afforded protection to the fishing fleet during the winter storms. The rich merchants built a magnificent church at Penmarch, emphasizing the maritime character of their town by some curious stone carvings of ships, that can still be seen. Then, within a few years, one disaster after another befell Penmarch. A storm of tremendous violence arose and an exceptionally high tide flooded the surrounding country. The harbour and most of the boats were destroyed. The cod disappeared from the coast and never returned. Civil wars broke out; bands of robbers and marauding troops ravaged and pillaged the villages. Penmarch was ruined. For centuries it remained desolate; the great manor houses and rich farms fell into ruins. The town shrank into little more than a small village huddling around the vast, cathedral-like church of Sainte-Nonna, as if expecting some fresh disaster to befall it. It was not until the sardine fishing was started less than a hundred years ago that Penmarch began to revive. But it is still a strange, forbidding sort of place: terrible in its grim austerity on a grey day in winter, when the wind is whistling through its streets and the ocean is thundering on the rocky shore.

Saint-Guénolé is a busy sardine port, facing the bay of Audierne and exposed to the fury of the western storms. All the male inhabitants are fishermen and all the women find employment in the sardine factories. It is a hard, cheerless, inhospitable place, where life is a particularly stern reality. A small harbour with a stone jetty affords but scant protection for the boats.

The lofty tower of the Phare d'Eckmühl, on the extreme end of the Pointe de Penmarch, is a prominent landmark for many miles out at sea. This lighthouse, 197 ft. high, was opened in 1897, and is said to be the most powerful lighthouse in the world. Its white light, flashing every five seconds, is visible thirty-five miles away. The tower was built with money left by the Marquise de Bloqueville in memory of her relation, Prince d'Eckmühl, one of Napoleon's marshals, with the idea that "les vies sauvées rachètent ainsi les larmes versées par la fatalité de la guerre"—in other words: to compensate for the innumerable lives lost in the campaigns in which Marshal Eckmühl took part.

Between Saint-Guénolé and the Pointe de Penmarch, right on the edge of the shore far away from any houses, stands a little granite chapel dedicated to "Notre-Dame de la Joie." It has stood here for centuries, exposed to the fury of every wind that blows, drenched by the waves and the spume during the storms of winter. No more desolate spot could well be imagined. One asks: Why the dedication, "Our Lady of Joy"?—should it not be "Our Lady of Sorrows"? But perhaps there is already enough tragedy and sadness in this dreary country of sand dunes and rocks, where life is such a perpetual struggle against the forces of nature. And so the mariners of Penmarch did right to turn our minds away from the sadness which is in this world, to her whom the Church bids us invoke as "Causa Nostræ Lætitiæ."

At *Kérity*, about two kilometres eastward from the Phare d'Eckmühl, is a small pier, affording shelter to the boats which belong here. As at Saint-Guénolé, all the inhabitants are engaged in the sardine fisheries.

Continuing along a low, sandy shore, behind which are marshes and potato-fields, after five kilometres we reach the more important

Saint-Guénolé and the Phare d'Eckmühl

fishing village of *Guilvinec*. It has a clean and prosperous appearance, largely due to its whitewashed houses and wide, open streets. There are numerous sardine factories, employing hundreds of women and girls, who parade the streets in their picturesque *Bigouden* costumes with tall white *coiffes* not unlike mitres in shape and appearance.

The port of Guilvinec is situated on a natural creek. It dries

GUILVINEC

at low water, and is difficult of approach, but within the break-water there is shelter during almost any weather. Mackerel fishing and trawling is also carried on by the Guilvinec fishermen, who land much of their catch at Lorient-Kéroman.

There is no other harbour anywhere on the coast of Finistère where the "ship lover" has such opportunities for studying the older kind of Breton fishing craft as at Guilvinec. Lying high and dry and dismantled in the upper part of the creek, is a veritable museum of every type of these vessels, abandoned to rot and decay. How long they will remain there I do not know, but when I last saw them in the summer of 1930, they were as numerous as ever.

The seafaring population of Guilvinec has a bad name for being unfriendly and even rude to strangers. My own experience has been exactly the opposite, and there are few places on the coast of Brittany of which I cherish such happy memories, or where the seamen were so ready and willing to talk to one. But other strangers have been equally fortunate, for, writing in the *Yachting Monthly* for June 1930 Mrs. D. F. Russell says: "The Guilvinic fishermen have a bad reputation with the islanders (Belle-Ile), who call them savages, but I must say that we seldom found them anything but courteous and pleasant to deal with. They are wonderful seamen and are also conspicuous for their personal cleanliness. I am not at all sure that this last is not the real cause of their unpopularity, for the ordinary Breton cannot understand why any normal human beings should strip to the waist and pour buckets of cold water over themselves every day and in all weathers."

Four kilometres beyond Guilvinec, situated on a small bay affording shelter to vessels in north and westerly winds, is the sardine port of *Lesconil*, dry at low water and possessing a small stone pier. The inhabitants of Lesconil are a strange, uncivilized race, with such a sinister reputation throughout Brittany that one sometimes wonders if they can be so bad as they are painted! Most of the fishermen are militant communists of an even more aggressive type than those of Douarnenez. Their hatred of religion sometimes shows itself in a startling fashion. I am told that on one occasion they marched into church on Sunday during the High Mass, singing the *Internationale*. I am also told that the Welsh Calvinistic Methodists have opened a mission in Lesconil. There is something rather odd in Communism and Calvinism banding together in this remote fishing village in Finistère in the hope of converting the inhabitants from the errors of Romanism! The Celt is never happy unless the pendulum swings from one extreme to the other; or as Anatole Le Braz puts it: "Hier chouan, demain anarchiste, sans cesse en réaction contre quelque chose ou contre quelqu'un."

Loctudy and *Ile-Tudy*, situated at the mouth of the River of Pont-l'Abbé, are two little ports each with a distinct character. The former in a delightfully wooded situation, does a steady trade in exporting vegetables. There is a good anchorage here, and alongside the quay you may often find one of the old sailing craft so familiar in the Breton coasting trade. Ile-Tudy lies on the other side of the river. It is not, strictly speaking, an island, but a narrow peninsula, with a population almost entirely made up of fishermen.

Six kilometres farther up the river we come to *Pont-l'Abbé*, capital of the "Bigouden country," famous for the curious costumes of its people. Coasting vessels put in here for cargoes of vegetables, the surrounding country being famous for its market-gardens.

Bénodet and *Sainte-Marine* lie opposite each other on the left and right banks of the mouth of the River Odet. This estuary, whose wooded shores are curiously reminiscent of Devonshire, is a popular centre with yachtsmen during the summer months. The Odet claims to be the "prettiest river in France," and for those who like this sort of placid scenery it must be almost perfection. Coasting vessels make their way up the river as far as the cathedral city of *Quimper*, alongside whose quay are generally to be found a British collier or a Scandinavian timber ship, unloading their cargo with an absence of rush or hurry that is soothing and restful to watch. Quimper can hardly be described as a seaport town, but it has bred many a famous seaman in its time, including De Kerguélen, the Antarctic explorer, who was born here in 1745.

Sainte-Marine is the home of a hardy race of fishermen, whose little cottages are scattered about near the shore embowered in trees. In one of the villas overlooking the river lives Monsieur de Thézac, the founder of the "Abris du Marin," or sailors' institutes, which have done so much to improve the social and moral conditions of the Breton fishermen all round the coast of Finistère. I have given further details of the "Abris du Marin" in another chapter.

Fifteen kilometres eastward of Bénodet, after passing *Beg-Meil*,

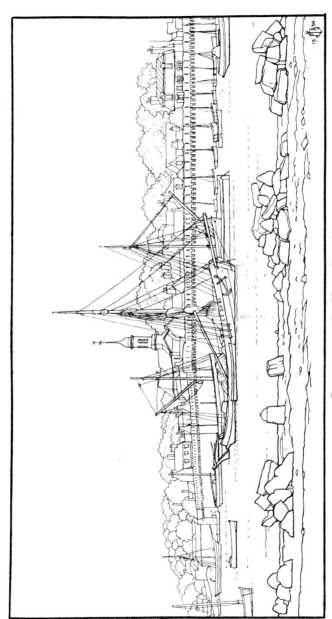

CONCARNEAU: "LA VILLE CLOSE"

opens out the Baie de la Forêt, on the farther side of which lies
the famous port of *Concarneau.* So often painted and sketched by
artists from every quarter of the globe, who flock here year after
year, Concarneau must be familiar to frequenters of art exhibitions
even if they have never been there in person. It is the *colour* of
Concarneau that lures the artist, for nowhere else in France, and
in few other places in Europe, does he find such opportunities for
a reckless orgy with all the most vivid pigments in his paint box.
There are the fishermen in their much - patched red jumpers,
trousers, and yellow oilskins. There are the gossamer-like blue
nets of the sardine boats. There are the kaleidoscopic hues of the
tunny boats, embracing the whole range of the spectrum. Added
to these you have the indefinable moisture-laden atmosphere of
Brittany, giving a depth and richness to colours which do not
exist in drier climates. Such is the charm of the place for the
artist. But Concarneau is not only an artists' colony. It is an
extremely busy fishing centre, with large factories for curing
sardines and tunny employing hundreds of women and girls.

The old town, or *ville close,* is built on an island entirely surrounded by fourteenth-century ramparts. In 1373 the English
besieged the town and captured it. A few years later Du Guesclin
sailed into the bay with his ships and forced the English to surrender
after a long resistance. In 1488 Concarneau became directly
subject to the King of France and, but for a few brief intervals,
remained under royal jurisdiction until the time of the Revolution.
As a result of its history, Concarneau has remained far more French
than Breton in character. Its fishermen speak French, not Breton,
as do those of all the surrounding villages.

The port of Concarneau opens to the south, and is protected on
the west by the land upon which the town is built. It consists of
an outer harbour, a large inner harbour, lying to the north of the
ramparts of the *ville close,* and a small fishing port at Passage-Lanriec
lying to the east. All the western part of the harbour is dry at low
water, so that the fishing vessels are then always aground. The
sardine and tunny boats land their fish on the quays of the old
harbour, where most of the hotels and shops are situated, and where

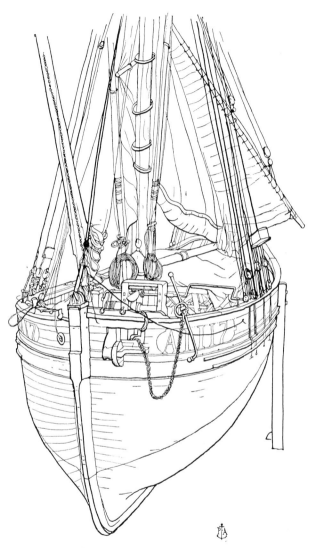

Tunny Boat at Concarneau

during the fishing season there is always a scene of great activity and excitement.

Apart from the fisheries Concarneau is of little importance. A certain amount of boat-building and repairing is carried on, and an occasional timber ship puts in from time to time. Taken as a whole, the maritime interests of the port are confined to the sardine and tunny fisheries. Yet at the same time, a certain amount of "white" fishing is carried on in small boats, chiefly for local consumption. On the shore, not far from the old chapel of Notre-Dame de Bon Secours, stands the aquarium, a laboratory of marine zoology, dependent on the museum in Paris.

The *Iles-des-Glénans* can be visited from Concarneau, where they are visible lying on the horizon about sixteen kilometres away to the south. They consist of some seven islands, low, bare, and treeless. The largest of them, *Penfret*, has a powerful lighthouse, and is inhabited by a few families of fisherfolk. On the *Ile Saint-Nicholas* is an old church and an *auberge* patronized in summer by day visitors from Concarneau, also a *vivier* for preserving lobsters and crayfish. *Cigogne* is occupied by a now abandoned fort which appears to date back several hundred years.

"It is difficult to ascribe to what is due the charm of these islands," wrote Captain Leslie Richardson in the *Yachting Monthly* for September 1912, "a charm strongly felt by the Bretons themselves. Their wildness and lack of convention seem to form a vent-hole for the savagery of the Breton character. Just as the young Corsican takes to the *maquis*, and the Basque to a smuggling trip across the Pyrénées, so the Breton of South Finistère sails off to the Glénans in order to rid himself of an oppressive civilization forced upon him by a misunderstanding government. . . . The Celt, ever a dreamer, is being driven to the far west; the islands of the Atlantic are his last sanctuary. Watch the gleam in old Biger's eye as he tells of the old wild days in the Glénans. Fierce fights, boats stove in, and cracked pates. A month's earnings spent in a night at the *auberge* on Saint-Nicholas, then a mere brandy shop. Marvellous catches of lobsters; rabbits caught in old sardine nets. Those were the wild old days."

DOUËLEN

Eight miles north of the Glénans lies the isolated *Ile-aux-Moutons* with its lighthouse, the only building here. There is no spring on the island and the lighthouse-keepers are dependent on rain for their supply of water.

Immediately facing the old town of Concarneau on its eastern side, and reached by a ferry, is the village of *Lanriec*, most of whose inhabitants are fishermen, and who, unlike those of Concarneau itself, speak Breton. There are sardine fisheries here, and a large fleet of boats.

Port-Manech, eighteen kilometres beyond Concarneau, is a small fishing centre of no great importance situated at the mouth of the River Aven. Three miles inland on the same river is *Pont-Aven*, more famous as an artists' colony than as a seaport, although a certain number of cargo-boats find their way up the narrow estuary of the river, between the wooded hills, and take on board vegetables and agricultural produce.

Brigneau and *Méryen* are insignificant hamlets of fishermen farther along the coast, both lying in sheltered creeks. So also is *Bélon*, at the mouth of the Riec; the latter is better known than the two former villages because of its oyster beds.

One of the most attractive little fishing ports that I know in Brittany is *Douëlen*, twelve kilometres east of Port-Manech, although it is seldom visited on account of its remote situation. In its sheltered creek, protected from the open sea, boats are safe in almost any weather. The sardine fisheries of Douëlen are very prosperous. During the season the creek is full of the type of craft I have shown in the accompanying drawing.

At *Le Pouldu* we reach the borders of Finistère, and across the River Laïta enter the *département* of Morbihan. Le Pouldu is only a secondary port; its sardine fisheries comparatively unimportant, although many boats take refuge here during easterly winds. In south and westerly winds it is much exposed.

Quimperlé, about fifteen kilometres up the River Laïta, is frequented by a few cargo-boats of small draught.

CHAPTER XV

AFTER Le Pouldu the coastline consists of low cliffs as far as the Pointe du Talud, ten kilometres in a south-easterly direction. Two kilometres beyond lies the little sardine port of *Lomener*, a favourite resort of the inhabitants of Lorient on account of its excellent fish restaurants. *Larmor*, another little fishing village, is situated at the entrance to the harbour of Lorient, formed of the estuary of the Rivers Blavet and Scorff.

Immediately opposite Larmor is *Port-Louis*, originally known as Locpéran. Its present name, given in honour of Louis XIII, only dates from 1616, when Richelieu ordered a new fort to be built here in place of the old one, which from 1590 to 1598 had been held by the Spaniards. Port-Louis is a quiet, sleepy little place that has gradually decayed since the foundation of Lorient in the seventeenth century. There is a small harbour here, some boat-building yards, and a certain number of fishing vessels.

Lorient, unlike Port-Louis, is a comparatively modern town. Before the year 1628 there seem to have been no houses here. In 1664 the Compagnie des Indes received its royal patent from Louis XIV, and a year or two later obtained possession of the land upon which now stands the town of Lorient, originally called "Lieu-d'Orient," because it was the headquarters of the company that did business with the Far East, the French equivalent to our own East India Company. Shipbuilding yards and quays were erected alongside the natural harbour afforded by the River Scorff just before it flows into the Blavet, the waters of the two rivers forming a magnificent anchorage for the frigates and schooners of the Compagnie des Indes. At the close of the seventeenth century there was no busier port in France. In 1719 the Compagnie des Indes was amalgamated with that of the Occident, which traded with the West Indies. The town's prosperity increased by leaps and bounds. But Colbert, in his capacity of Minister of the Marine, began to see that Lorient might be useful to the Government as a naval base. He arranged for ships to be built there, and eventually the Compagnie des Indes found themselves driven out of the port they had caused to be built at such enormous expense.

In 1746 the British fleet under Admiral Lestock embarked troops at Le Pouldu, and proceeded to attack Lorient, but was obliged to retire. A permanent souvenir of this British attempt to capture Lorient can be seen to-day in the cannon-ball firmly wedged into the walls of the Chapelle de la Congrégation at the corner of the rue de la Patrie. Louis XV allowed England to gain possession of the French colonies in India, the Compagnie des Indes was broken up, and in 1770 the town and dockyard of Lorient passed into the hands of the State.

To-day Lorient really consists of two ports, the *port militaire*, which includes the dockyard situated on the right bank of the Scorff, and secondly the *port de commerce*, of more recent construction, formed out of the Anse de Faouëdec. It includes an *avant-port* with quays on either side and a wet dock. Lorient does a regular trade in exporting pit-props, and coal is an important import.

At *Lorient-Kéroman* you have an opportunity to study the Breton fisheries in their most up-to-date conditions. You should make an effort to get down to the harbour not later than 6 a.m. in order to watch the arrival of the great steam trawlers laden with every sort of fish.

If you turn into the spacious and well-equipped Maison du Marin, even at this early hour, you will probably find its restaurant full of stalwart fishermen who have come off their boats and are eating their *cotriade*, the traditional Breton dish made of fish and potatoes, or drinking steaming bowls of coffee. Mingling with them are coopers, salesmen, packers, buyers, and all the other employees of this great fish port.

Make your way on to the vast covered-in quays alongside which the trawlers are unloading their catch; the baskets and boxes of

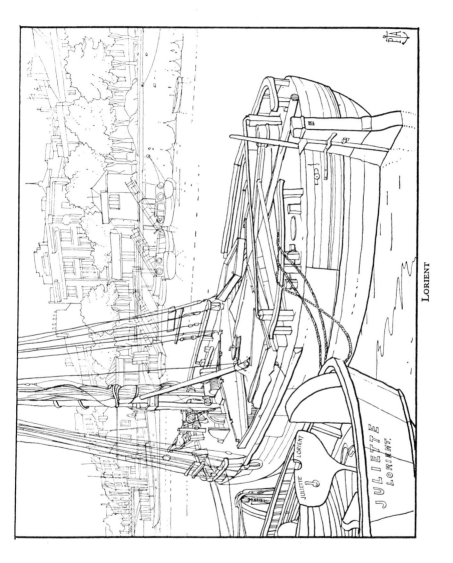

LORIENT

fish are being hurried away in every direction on little motor-driven trucks. Here you will find specimens of almost every edible fish that can be caught off the shores of Europe: great flat turbots and rays, black-bellied dogfish, long slithery eels, gurnards, sturgeons, all lying in rows waiting to be sold and dispatched by rail to every part of France and even beyond. Some distance farther on, piled up high on tables, are masses of silver-blue mackerel, shimmering beneath the glare of electric light. Lobsters, crabs, and crayfish, always in much demand in France, are also a prominent feature of this huge fish market.

But there are other fish even more interesting and curious, for instance the red mullet with their spiky fins and long moustaches; the speckled *roussette*, whose leopard-like skin is made into handbags; the smelts, which the Lorientais call *prêteaux*, or "little priests," from the contents of whose bladder artificial pearls are formed; and many another strange fish whose English names I cannot recall.

Wherever you turn there are silent and attentive groups of buyers watching and listening to the strident-voiced salesman, who keeps his eye on one and all, ready to catch the slightest movement of their lips if they decide to bid. There are old women who go on knitting unperturbed by their surroundings, young *mareyeuses* in their gay red aprons: a terribly businesslike crowd whose only preoccupation seems to be that of buying or selling fish.

At the other side of the port you will find a basin full of sailing and motor vessels, the quays swarming with fishermen from almost every port in southern Brittany. Here you are nearly sure to knock up against some old friends from Concarneau, Guilvinec, Belle-Ile, Le Croisic, La Turballe, or even distant Camaret.

Such is an impression of Lorient-Kéroman, the most up-to-date fishing port in France.

Hennebont is another typical inland port, ten kilometres from Lorient up the River Blavet. So deep is the channel that ships of up to fifteen hundred tons can proceed as far as the railway viaduct a short distance from the town. Alongside the quays you will nearly always find one or two smaller craft being loaded with pit-props from the neighbouring forests. Over five hundred years

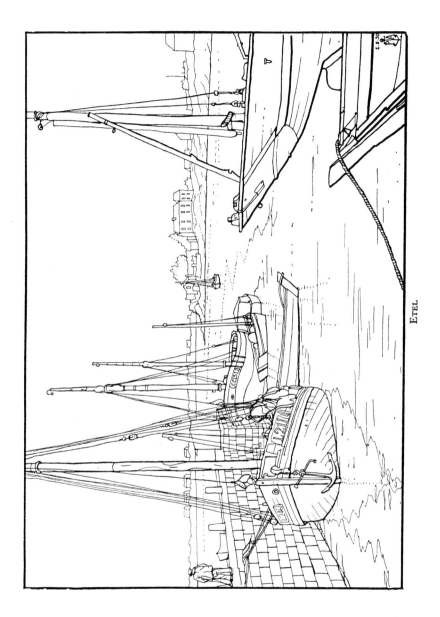

ETEL

ago a fleet of English ships sailed up the River Blavet and prevented the Breton troops from having to surrender to the French. The castle of Hennebont was garrisoned by English from 1344 to 1372 when they were driven out by Du Guesclin.

The *Ile-de-Groix* is generally reached by taking the little steamer

TRAWLERS AT LORIENT-KÉROMAN

that runs daily from Lorient, the passage occupying about an hour. Groix is eight kilometres long with an average breadth of from two to three kilometres, i.e. about the same size as Ouessant, but with a very different character and appearance. For Groix, although treeless, has a smiling and pleasant aspect. "Qui voit Groix, voit sa joie," says the old Breton proverb, and rightly so; it is essentially a joyous and happy little island. On the north side there are numerous sheltered bays, two harbours, *Port-Tudy* and *Port-Maria*, the former with a sheltered anchorage formed of two stone jetties, at certain seasons of the year crowded with a fleet of tunny boats, of which Groix owns the greatest number of any port in Brittany. Indeed the Grésillons, as the inhabitants are called, can claim the honour of having introduced tunny fishing to their fellow fishermen on this part of the coast. Port-Maria, lying to the south-east, opens seawards, but affords good anchorage in west and north-west winds. The five thousand inhabitants of Groix are almost all engaged in either the sardine or the tunny fisheries. Their whitewashed houses, scattered over the island or grouped together in villages, are embowered in vegetation of a sub-tropical character, figs and laurustinus being quite common.

It was frequently attacked by the English and Dutch during the seventeenth and eighteenth centuries. In 1696 the allied vessels of these two nations made a landing here and destroyed most of the houses. An amusing story is told, how on one occasion, when the British ships were hovering off the coast, the *curé* of the island had the brilliant idea to dress up the inhabitants in red petticoats belonging to the women and to arm them with sticks and brooms. When seen from a distance they had the appearance of a large army of soldiers encamped on the cliffs. So the British admiral thought it prudent to sail away, not wishing to risk a defeat.

On Saint John the Baptist's Day, 24th June, the annual Pardon, or blessing of the sea, takes place, a most picturesque sight, details of which are given in another chapter.

The Grésillons and their charming little island really deserve much more space than I have been able to devote to them, for there are few places on the coasts of southern Brittany where one would so gladly linger.

Continuing in a south-easterly direction along the coast from Port-Louis, the next port we come to is *Etel*, famous for its sardine factories and fleet of tunny boats. If it were not for the sand bar that obstructs the mouth of the river, and the dangerous currents,

Etel might have developed much more than it has done. There
is only a small harbour here.

The peninsula of Quiberon, about nine kilometres beyond the
mouth of the River Etel, projects into the sea for some fifteen
kilometres, its greatest breadth being three kilometres, often much
less. The surface is bare and treeless; the west coast famous for its
rocky cliffs.

There are three fishing centres on the peninsula, *Portivy*, *Port-
Haliguen*, and *Port-Maria*, the last being the only one that is of any
real importance. It is situated at the extreme end of the Presqu'île
de Quiberon. The regular steamer service for Belle-Ile starts
from here. It consists of a sheltered harbour formed of two stone
jetties and a detached breakwater. Except in heavy seas from the
westward Port-Maria can be entered in most weathers. The sardine
factories of Quiberon employ a large number of persons, and during
the fishing season the harbour is crowded with boats.

The little harbour of *Le Pô* is only frequented by a few fishing
craft. It is within a short distance of the famous stones of Carnac,
and faces the Bay of Quiberon, the scene of the naval battle between
the French and the English in 1746, and where Admiral Sir John
Warren landed his troops in 1795 in the forlorn hope of restoring
the Bourbons.

Belle-Ile is the largest of the Breton islands and has a well-deserved
reputation for the picturesque character of its scenery. But I must
admit that in recent years Belle-Ile has become rather sophisticated
and over-exploited as a holiday resort, and if one has already made
the acquaintance of Ouessant and Sein, Belle-Ile is just a little
disappointing. There is a regular service of steamers from Quiberon
to Le Palais, and numerous hotels which cater for the crowds of
visitors who flock here in summer.

The island, which contains about 6,800 inhabitants, is six miles
from the mainland, seventeen kilometres long and from five to nine
kilometres broad. On the north the coast is broken up by several
secluded bays. On the south the rugged coast scenery quite lives
up to the reputation it has acquired through intensive advertising
—those famous granite cliffs whose photographs confront one in

Le Palais, Belle-Ile

the carriages of the Paris-Orléans railway, and upon which Sarah Bernhardt built herself a château.

The history of the island is full of exciting events. Its situation rendered it liable to constant attacks by sea from any hostile fleet that happened to be in the neighbourhood. The original owners of the island seem to have been the Comtes de Cornouaille, by whom it was given to the abbey of Sainte-Croix at Quimperlé in the ninth century. In order to defend it against frequent assaults by pirates the monks erected the first fortifications here. In 1548 an English fleet of thirty-six ships attempted to land on the island but were repulsed. Twenty-four years later another attack was made by sea, the inhabitants surrendered, and the English captors remained three weeks. In 1673 the Dutch under Van Tromp managed to land, but were afterwards driven off. In 1746 the English made several unsuccessful efforts to take the island. In 1761 Admiral Keppel with a force of twenty thousand men attacked Le Palais, whose inhabitants after a brave defence of thirty-eight days were eventually obliged to surrender. The English remained masters of Belle-Ile for two years, when it was returned to France after the Treaty of Paris, in exchange for the French colony of Acadie in Canada, many of whose settlers returned to Europe and settled on Belle-Ile. In 1795 Admiral Ellison, during the ill-fated expedition at Quiberon, attempted to land here. During its chequered history Belle-Ile has changed owners several times. From 1720 to 1759 it belonged to the Compagnie des Indes, of which I have spoken in my account of Lorient.

Le Palais is the capital of the island. It is a busy and picturesque little town facing the mainland; its harbour, always crowded with boats during the fishing season, consists of an *avant-port* with two long stone jetties, a wet dock, and inner basin. A certain amount of agricultural produce is exported here.

Sauzon, seven kilometres north-west of Le Palais, is situated on the west side of a sheltered harbour, dry at low water, with a large fleet of fishing-boats. The inhabitants are of a different race to the rest of the islanders; the name Sauzon ("Saxon") indicating a Germanic origin.

GOULPHAR, BELLE-ILE

Loc-Maria is a tranquil village of fisherfolk with a little secluded harbour, lying on the south-east side of the island. Yachtsmen, who are very frequent visitors to Belle-Ile in the summer months, will all remember the charming and romantically situated harbour of *Goulphar*, just below the powerful lighthouse, whose rays are visible twenty-three miles. "The Breton fishermen know it, and on a summer's night you may find as many as thirty boats lying here, from Guilvinec, Concarneau, Lorient, Auray, and even far distant Camaret, not to mention the tiny craft belonging to the local peasant fisherfolk, for here, in everything but a gale from the south-west, is perfect shelter. Deep water, clean and spacious anchorage, a spring near at hand, together with a little hotel where some very drinkable *vin rouge* may be procured and where the sybarite may seek hot baths and the flesh-pots, and half a mile away a general stores, bring it as close to perfection as the heart of man can desire." [1]

From Belle-Ile one can hire a boat and sail across to the seldom-visited islands of *Hoëdik* and *Houat* (the *Cane* and the *Caneton* as they are familiarly called), the two islands geologically forming part of the peninsula of Quiberon. Hoëdik is a bare desolate spot, four kilometres long, flat and barren, with a small harbour among the rocks, and a village of rather neglected-looking houses, close by to a church. The island reminds one in many ways of Sein; the ground is divided up *ad infinitum* among the 280 inhabitants, and manages to produce rye, oats, and potatoes. All the men are seafarers and the work of the island is done by the women. Houat is rather larger than its neighbour, but has about the same population, and is equally desolate and featureless, except that the cliffs of red granite possess a certain rugged grandeur. A curious old menhir surmounted by a cross is pointed out to visitors. In one of its crevices the fisherfolk have placed an image of Notre-Dame de Bon Secours. These two islands can be also reached from Quiberon by means of a smack that sails three times a week with mails and provisions.

La Trinité-sur-Mer, lying on the west side of the estuary of the

[1] D. F. Russell, *Yachting Monthly*, May 1930, p. 23.

Crach, is a picturesque and charmingly situated fishing village, with productive oyster beds.

The *Golfe-du-Morbihan*, a shallow inland sea, dotted with over two hundred islands, is of comparatively recent formation. Two thousand years ago it may have been a low-lying plain. It is entered by a narrow channel, on either side of which are the two villages of *Locmariaquer* and *Port-Navalo*. The majority of their

"Chasse-Marée" on the Golfe-du-Morbihan

inhabitants are fishermen. Port-Navalo possesses a sheltered anchorage, protected by a small stone pier. The most important islands in the Golfe-du-Morbihan are the *Ile-aux-Moines* and *Arz*, whose inhabitants are seafarers, nearly all the men of the Ile-aux-Moines serving in the mercantile marine. They are said to be of Spanish origin, descended from the Spanish troops who were garrisoned on this part of the coast of Morbihan in the sixteenth century. Coasting vessels, laden with coal and timber, are frequently to be found moored against the quays of *Auray* and *Vannes*, both reached by tortuous channels from the Golfe-du-Morbihan.

About two kilometres from Port-Navalo, already mentioned, is the village of *Arzon*, famous for the vow made by forty-two of its sailors in 1673, on the eve of sailing to fight the Dutch, that if they were victorious they would make an annual pilgrimage to the shrine of Sainte-Anne-d'Auray. Ever since they have remembered this vow, sailing up to Auray in their boats at Whitsuntide: a picturesque sight that is worth seeing.

Beyond the Golfe-du-Morbihan the flat coastline stretches away eastwards for thirty kilometres or so until one arrives at the mouth of the River Vilaine. *Billiers* and *Penerf*, situated on either side of the estuary, are the only ports that are worth mentioning, and neither of them are of any commercial importance. *Tréhiguier*, about fourteen kilometres from the mouth of the Vilaine, affords a sheltered anchorage, and *La-Roche-Bernard*, eighteen kilometres farther inland, has a certain amount of trade in pit props and agricultural produce.

CHAPTER XVI

LOIRE-INFÉRIEURE—PIRIAC TO NANTES

SOUTH of the River Vilaine, at the far end of a peninsula facing north-west, lies the fishing village of *Piriac*, of small importance commercially, and dangerous of approach in rough weather. Some protection is afforded by a stone pier. *La Turballe*, which lies about four kilometres south-east of Piriac, is even more exposed to the sea. It is a busy, straggling village of hardy fisherfolk, all of whom, both men and women, are employed in the sardine fisheries. My sketch of La Turballe shows the harbour formed of two stone piers, and some of the older type of boats still to be found here. In a south-westerly gale it is almost impossible for any craft to enter the harbour.

The *Ile-de-Bâtz*, upon which the ports of Le Croisic and Le Pouliguen are situated, was a real island at one time. The salt marshes which now lie on its northern side originally formed a channel, separating the Ile-de-Bâtz from the mainland. The whole district abounds in Gallo-Roman remains, and a tradition related by various chroniclers would locate here those legendary islands inhabited by a race of women who worshipped Bacchus, and who never allowed a man to land upon their shores: they themselves making occasional visits to the mainland.[1]

Somewhere in this neighbourhood lay the "harbour of the Two Crows" (*Portus Duorum Corvorum*) and the *Portus Brivates* of classical geographers. Even in the days of the Romans these shores were the home of fishermen and sailors. The Ile-de-Bâtz may be said, therefore, to possess a maritime history going back over two thousand years.

Le Croisic, nowadays a busy sardine port and of some importance

---

[1] Ptolemy, II, viii, 6; Marcien, II, 21; Strabo, liv., IV, iv, 6. See also Dionysius Perieg. *Geogr. min.*, II, v, 570–9.

commercially, is built on the inner side of this granite peninsula facing north, overlooking the salt marshes of Le Grand Trait. It is first mentioned in the sixth century. Its inhabitants, quite different in appearance and mentality to any others in Brittany, would appear to be of Saxon or Scandinavian origin.

The town was fortified and surrounded by walls about 1355. During the sixteenth century Le Croisic governed itself like a little republic. It was not until the reign of Louis XIV that it was deprived of its independence. In 1759 the French fleet was defeated off the shore by the English, who sailed in and bombarded the town for three days.

There is no town in Brittany, with perhaps the exception of Saint-Malo, that has such an unbroken connection with the sea than Le Croisic, and it has been the home of many famous seafarers. During the seventeenth and eighteenth centuries a fleet of vessels was fitted out here every year for the Newfoundland cod fisheries.

The port of Le Croisic is made up of an *avant-port* protected by a stone jetty, long quays, against which are generally moored a few coasting vessels as well as fishing-boats, and some curious artificial islands known as *chambres*, which also afford moorings for the fishing fleet.

Le Pouliguen ("Poul-Guen"=white port; so called from the white sand-dunes which surround it) is built on the right bank of a little stream that drains the salt marshes. Although it cannot boast the antiquity of Le Croisic, it has been a fishing centre for many centuries. Within recent years, however, its maritime character has been greatly lost, and it is rapidly becoming a popular bathing resort. My drawing of Le Pouliguen gives an idea of the type of fishing-boat still found here, most of which are engaged in trawling for whitefish, many of them landing their catch at Lorient-Kéroman.

The Loire has the unenviable reputation of being the most capricious and the most troubled river in France. Its waters are generally yellow and turgid. Sometimes they are no more than a feebly trickling stream, and other times a violent, rushing torrent. The river is always blocking up its bed with constantly shifting banks of sand, which, together with the rapid currents and frequent

LA TURBALLE

floods, are a constant source of danger to navigation. The characteristic feature of the Loire is the great width of its bed, everywhere broken up by innumerable islands and channels through which, for the greater part of the year, there is never enough water.

Nantes, the *Portus Namnetum* of the Romans, is built on a group of these islands in a strategical position at the junction of the Loire,

LE POULIGUEN

Erdre, and Sèvre, thirty miles from the sea. In Gallo-Roman days Nantes was not an important city, merely a *vicus portensis*. In the first century A.D. it did a certain amount of commerce in precious metals: gold and tin being found in considerable quantities in Gaul at that time. The maritime development of Nantes may be said to be due to Saint Felix, the bishop who in 560 built a canal to link up the Loire and the Erdre.

But it was not until after the discovery of America that Nantes

NANTES

began to take its place as one of the chief ports in France. It opened up commercial relations with Flanders, Holland, Scandinavia, and Ireland. Almost every day a vessel would be sailing for some Spanish port, especially for Bilbao, with which Nantes had formed a definite commercial agreement as early as 1491, the management of which was under the control of the Confrérie de la Contractation. There was no more cosmopolitan city in France. On the quays of Nantes one heard spoken almost every language of Europe. Colonies of Spanish, Dutch, and Irish merchants had their home here. Five mayors of Nantes in the seventeenth century were of Spanish origin. Mercantile families used to send their sons to Spain, Portugal, Holland, to learn the language of these countries.

Its sea-borne trade developed, not only with America but with the Far East. Merchants from Nantes were to be found in Canada, Louisiana, Peru, Newfoundland, and the West Indies. In 1715 no less than eighty-seven ships were trading with the West Indies. They generally sailed in November and December, the crossing of the Atlantic taking about fifty days. They returned home in June. Some vessels made two trips a year. Sugar brought back from the West Indies was refined at Nantes and exported all over Europe.

But the prosperity of Nantes was due far more to the slave trade than anything else. The seventeenth- and eighteenth-century merchants used to fit out whole fleets of vessels for this purpose. Sailing for the coast of Guinea, their captains would procure by barter shiploads of negroes—often as many as seven or eight hundred poor wretches would be crowded together on board, in conditions that defy description. Many of them died before reaching the West Indies. The rest were sold or exchanged for rum, spices, cocoa, sugar, and coffee. Between 1750 and 1790 from ten to twelve thousand slaves were transported annually from the Guinea Coast to the West Indies. With the wealth gained by the slave trade the merchants of Nantes were able to build those palatial mansions which are still standing, facing the Quai de la Fosse, no longer in their former glory, but sadly decayed, and turned into flats and tenements, the abode of the lowest type of humanity to be found in the "sailor-town" of an old seaport.

By the year 1704 Nantes had risen to the rank of the first port in France, with a fleet of 1332 vessels.   In 1790 no less than 2500 ships were registered here: 259 "long-courriers," 271 "grands caboteurs," 725 "petits caboteurs," and 1300 "barques."

However, the city did not rise to this state of prosperity without having to fight for it.   Its fleet was often attacked by sea; enemies were always to be found cruising about the mouth of the Loire, lying in wait for some richly laden vessel on her way home from the West Indies or the Far East.   To protect themselves the Nantes merchants had to organize a regular service of armed convoys. The corsairs of Nantes became almost as famous as those of Saint-Malo, among whom the names of Cassard, Crabosse, and Vié are still remembered.   Jacques Cassard, who began life as a fisher boy off Newfoundland, eventually became one of the greatest seamen of France.   His statue adorns the façade of the Bourse at Nantes. He was much more than a mere corsair; he was the successful leader of great maritime expeditions—for did he not capture Antigua, Montserrat, Surinam, Curaçao, Cape Verde Islands, and Essequibo, to mention but a few of his exploits?   A romantic story of which, I regret, lack of space forbids me to give further details. And yet this fine old sea-dog was allowed to die in prison and in penury, the victim of political squabbles.

With the suppression of the Slave Trade after the Revolution the fortunes of Nantes began to wane.   Ships grew bigger; they could not venture so far up the river; many of them unloaded their cargoes at Paimbœuf or Saint-Nazaire.   And with the opening of the first dock at the latter port in 1856 the death-blow to Nantes was struck.

The city has changed character in consequence.   Nowadays Nantes has little of what one may describe as a "maritime atmosphere."   Rather is it a big, busy provincial city, reminiscent of Lyons or Toulouse, far less suggestive of the presence of the sea than even Rouen or Bordeaux.   But wandering along the Quai de la Fosse, past the Pont Transbordeur (which I have shown in the sketch

NANTES

made from the corner of the Ile Gloriette), you will still come across
a number of tramp steamers, loading or unloading their cargoes.
A large area is covered with sheds, warehouses, and cranes, and on
the river itself are a never-ending procession of barges, lighters,
and tugs.   On the water-front you can take your choice of innumerable *débits* and cafés that still exist for the benefit of sailormen.
There are ships' chandlers too, and overhanging all, the great
domed church of Notre-Dame de Bon Port—that *ought* to be full
of ex-voto models of ships and pictures of preservation from storms
and shipwrecks, but which is merely cold, bare, respectable, and
bourgeois, and not at all the sort of place that the old-time sea rover
of Nantes would have felt at home in, although it may appeal to his
present-day successor, if he ever enters its frigid Greco-Roman
portico.

Nantes has become much more a city that controls shipping rather
than a seaport: that is the essential difference.   And that is why,
I take it, it has so little to offer to the "ship lover" who visits it
to-day, hoping to recapture something of the glorious past.

In addition to the enormous length of quays at Nantes and its
suburb *Chantenay*, there are large shipbuilding works on both banks
of the river.

Between Nantes and the sea, a distance of forty-seven kilometres,
one passes the six following ports (right bank) *Couëron, La Basse-Indre,*
and *Saint-Nazaire*; (left bank) *Indret, Le Pellerin,* and *Paimbœuf.*

Indre is made up of the three adjacent towns of Indret, La Basse-
Indre, and La Haute-Indre.   The latter is a village mainly
inhabited by fishermen; La Basse-Indre and Indret, on the contrary, are busy industrial towns with large engineering and shipbuilding works.

Couëron at one time was a sort of free port of Nantes, being largely
frequented by Dutch ships.   To-day it is mainly an industrial town
with iron foundries and factories.

Le Pellerin is of no great importance, and *Paimbœuf,* which a
hundred years ago seemed likely to develop into a prosperous
seaport, has sunk back into a sleepy little village since the creation
of Saint-Nazaire.   From 1830 to 1860 its shipbuilding yards turned

out a large number of "voiliers" and "goëlettes," but to-day they are most of them closed and abandoned.

Saint-Nazaire is a town of quite recent foundation. Sixty years ago the promontory at the mouth of the Loire upon which it is built was little more than a small village, inhabited by a few pilots and fishermen. Yet the history of Saint-Nazaire goes back for nearly two thousand years, for it is built on the site of a Gallo-Roman town called Corbilon. During the fourteenth and fifteenth centuries there was a strongly fortified castle here, held by the dukes of Brittany. Later on the place became known as Port-Nazaire. The first dock here was built in 1830, for the purpose of affording better protection for the pilot-boats and with no intention of creating a rival to Nantes. But with the introduction of steam, the gradual increase in size of vessels, and the constant shifting of the bed of the Loire, the opportunities that Saint-Nazaire offered for a commercial port were soon realized. In 1842 the foundations of the present *bassin à flot* were laid, and it was opened in 1856. Since then another wet dock of more than double the area, the Bassin de Penhoët, has been built, and to-day Saint-Nazaire has become the chief base of the Compagnie Générale Transatlantique, commonly known as "La Transat." Modern Saint-Nazaire is curiously reminiscent of a typical American seaport town with its up-to-date docks and broad, straight streets. Moreover it has all the familiar characteristic features of the twentieth-century sailor town: the cafés, bars, dancing saloons, and cinemas. Loafing around the "sailor town" quarter, right and left of the rue Thiers, and in those queer ramshackle streets off the place du Bassin, are crowds of seamen from off the big liners and tramp steamers; the same type as you meet in Liverpool, Buenos Aires, San Francisco, or Shanghai. Most of them are Bretons, although from their appearance they might belong to any part of France or to any nation, so little is there to distinguish the modern seaman in the mercantile marine of one country from another.

On approaching Saint-Nazaire from the sea one notices by the shore a bronze statue of a soldier standing on an eagle with outstretched wings. This monument records the fact that during the war Saint-Nazaire was "Base One" of the American Expeditionary Force and its streets were full of the United States sailors and soldiers. Saint-Nazaire has always had a warm place in its affections for Americans; indeed it owes its very life and existence to its commerce with the New World, and, as I have already remarked, in its lay-out and appearance is far more suggestive of a transatlantic seaport town than any other city I know in Europe.

We began our survey of the Breton ports at Saint-Malo, the city of the corsairs. We conclude it at Saint-Nazaire, the city of the modern ocean liners. Lying between the two are to be found every type of seafarer, every class of vessel. In these pages I have tried to convey something of the characteristic features of both: the human element, the lives and surroundings of the men themselves, the ships in which they sail. It is no more than a hasty sketch, a mere impression, for the story of the mariners of Brittany is too vast a subject to be dealt with as it deserves within the compass of one small volume.

BIBLIOGRAPHY

A. General Works

Baring-Gould, S., and Fisher, J. *Lives of the British Saints.* 1907. 4 vols.
Brekilien, Y. *La vie quotidienne des paysans en Bretagne au XIX⁰ siècle.* 1966.
Brekilien, Y. *Prestiges du Finistère* (Paris, Ed. France-Empire 1969).
Buffet, H.-F. *En haute Bretagne.* 1954.
Callaux, C. *La Basse Bretagne, étude de géographie humaine.* 1907.
Cambry, J. *Voyage dans le Finistère en 1794 et 1795.*
Chardronnet, J. *Histoire de Bretagne.* 1965.
De la Borderie et Pocquet. *L'Histoire de Bretagne.* 1896–1904.
Delumeau, J. (ed.) *Histoire de la Bretagne.* 1969.
Delumeau, J. (ed.) *Documents de l'Histoire de la Bretagne.* 1971.
Dupuis, A. et Coant, F. *Au beau pays de Bretagne.* 1953.
Gautier, M. *La Bretagne Centrale.* 1947.
Giot, P.-R., L'Helgouach, J., et Briard, J. *La Bretagne, préhistoire et proto-histoire.* 1962.
Giot, P.-R. *Menhirs et dolmens, monuments mégalithiques de Bretagne.* 1970.
Giot, P.-R. *La Bretagne avant l'histoire.* 1971.
Gourvil, F. *Langue et littérature bretonnes.* 1968.
Guerin. *Histoire maritime.* 1851–2. 6 vols.
Langlois, C. V. *L'Histoire de Bretagne.* 1891.
Le Gallo, Y. *Bretagne* (Paris, Arthuad, 1969).
Le Goffic, C. *La Bretagne* (Paris, Hachette).
Le Grand, P. A. *Vie des Saints de la Bretagne Armorique.* Edition Thomas, Abgrall et Peyron. 1901.
Le Lannou, M. *Géographie de la Bretagne.* 1950–2. 2 vols.
Lentheric, C. *Côtes et Port Francais.* 1901–6. 2 vols.
Les Guides Bleus: *Bretagne.* 1930.
Les Guides Bleus: *Bretagne.* 1972.
Levron, J. *Petite histoire de Bretagne.* 1946.
Musset, R. *La Bretagne* (Paris, A. Colin, 1938).
Ogee, L. *La Dictionnaire historique et géographique de la Province de Bretagne.* Edition Marteville et Varin. 1843. 2 vols.
Poisson, H. *Histoire de Bretagne.* 1971. 5th ed.
Ports maritimes de la France. Ministère des Travaux Publics. 1874–1900. 8 vols.
Queffelec, H. *Bretagne* (Paris, Hachette. Albums des Guides Bleus, 1956); *Bretagne intérieure* (ibid., 1956); *Ports de pêche en Bretagne* (ibid., 1960); *La Bretagne des Parsons* (ibid., 1962).

QUEFFELEC, H. *Franche et secrète Bretagne* (Grenoble, Arthaud, 1960); *En Bretagne: Tregor-Leon* (ibid., 1952).
SEBILLOT, P.-Y. *La Bretagne pittoresque et légendaire.* 1924.
VALLAUX, C., WAQUET, H., CHASSE, C., et DUPOUY, A. *Horizons de France: Bretagne.* 1963.
WAQUET, H. *Tableau de la Bretagne* (Paris, Alpina, 1957).
WAQUET, H. *Art Breton.* 1960.
WAQUET, H. et DE SAINT-JOUAN, R. *Histoire de la Bretagne.* 1970. 5th ed.

B. MODERN WORKS OF A TOPOGRAPHICAL, HISTORICAL, OR LITERARY CHARACTER

CARADEC, T. *Autour des Iles Bretonnes.* n.d.
CHEVRILLON, A. *Derniers reflets à l'Occident.* 1925. L'Enchantement Breton. 1928.
DE GALZAIN, M. *Golfe du Morbihan* (Chateaulin, Le Doare); *Quiberon-Carnac* (ibid.).
DERVEAUX, D. *De la Côte d'Emeraude à Broceliande par la Rance.* 1959–60. 2 vols.
DUPONT, E. *Les Corsaires chez eux.* 1929. *L'Aumonier des Corsaires.* n.d.
DUPOUY, A. *Brest et Lorient* (Paris, Dunod, 1926).
DURAND, A. *Nantes dans la France de l'Ouest* (Paris, Plon, 1941).
ELDER, M. *Jacques Cassard, Corsaire de Nantes.* 1930.
GAUTHIER, J. S. *La Bretagne, Sites, Arts et Costumes* (Paris, Librairie des Arts decoratifs, 1929); *Croix et calvaires de Bretagne* (Paris, Plon, 1944); *Calvaires bretons* (Grenoble, Arthaud, 1950); *Tro-Briez, Pèlerinage aux vieux sanctuaires bretons* (Paris, Librairie celtique, 1950).
LE BRAZ, A. *Iles bretonnes (Belle-Isle, Sein)* (Paris, Calmann-Levy, 1935).
LE GOFFIC, C. *L'Ame Bretonne.* n.d. *Sur la Côte.* n.d. *Ames d'Occident.* n.d.
LE LANNOU, M. *Ports et havres de Brest* (Paris, Ed. des Belles-Lettres, 1913).
MEVEL, P. *Les Seigneurs de la Mer.* 1927.
QUEFFELEC, H. *Brest* (Chateaulin, La Doare).
SOUVESTRE, E. *Derniers Bretons. Souvenirs d'un Bas-Breton. Le Foyer Breton.*
VALERY, P. Mer, Marines, Marins. 1930.
VERCEL, R. *Saint-Malo et l'âme malouine* (Paris, Albin Michel, 1948); *La Rance* (Paris, Arc-en-Ciel, 1945).

C. FOLK-LORE

BOUET, A. et PERRIN, O. *Briez-Izel ou la Vie des Bretons de l'Armorique* (Paris, Tchou, 1970).
BUFFET, H.-F. *En Bretagne morbihannaise* (Grenoble, Arthaud, 1948); *En Haute-Bretagne, coutumes et traditions* (Paris, Librairie Celtique, 1954).
DE LANGLAIS, X. *Le Roman du roi Arthur, les Compagnons de la Table Ronde* (Paris, Piazza, 1965).
HERPIN, E. *La Côte d'Emeraude.* 1894.
JOHNSON, W. B. *Folk Tales of Brittany.*

La Landelle, G. *Moeurs maritimes.* 1867.
Le Braz, A. *La Légende de la Mort chez les Bretons. Au Pays des Pardons.*
Le Braz, A. *La Légende de la mort chez les Bretons armoricains* (Paris, Champion, 1946); *Vieilles histoires du Pays Breton* (Paris, Calmann-Levy, 1931); *Le Théâtre celtique* (Paris, Calmann-Levy, 1905); *Au Pays des pardons* (Rennes, Cailliere, 1894).
Le Goffic, C. *L'Ame bretonne* (Paris, Champion, 1924).
Markale, J. *L'épopée celtique en Bretagne* (Paris, Payot).
Sebillot, P. *Le Folk-Lore des Pêcheurs.* 1901. *Contes de Marins.* 1882. *Légendes, croyances et superstitions de la mer.* 1886–7.
Sebillot, P.-Y. *Le Folklore de la Bretagne* (Paris, Maisonneuve et Larose, 1968, 2 vols).
Souvestre, E. *Le foyer breton* (Paris, Vigneau, 1947); *Contes de Bretagne* (Paris, Le Liseron, 1946).

D. Fiction

Dupouy, A. *Pêcheurs bretons* (Paris, De Boccard, 1920); *Face au couchant* (Paris' La Renaissance du Livre, 1932); *Le chemin de ronde*; *L'Homme de la Palud* (Paris, L'Illustration, 1921).
Elder, M. *Le Peuple de la Mer.* n.d.
Herpin, E. *Terreneuvas.* 1896.
Kellermann, B. *La Mer.* 1930.
Le Braz, A. *Contes du soleil et de la brume* (Paris, Delagrave, 1925); *La Terre du Passe* (Paris, Calmann-Levy, 1926); *Pâques d'Islande* (ibid., 1926); *Le gardien du feu* (Paris, Nelson, 1929).
Le Goffic, C. *Bretagne* (Paris, De Boccard, 1927); *Passions celtes* (Paris, La Renaissance du Livre, 1925); *L'Abbesse de Guerande* (Paris, Plon, 1927); *L'illustre Bobinet* (Paris, Plon, 1925); *La Payse* (Paris, Ferenczi, 1930); *Le Crucifie de Keralies* (Paris, Plon, 1927); *Morgane* (ibid., 1933); *L'Erreur de Florence* (Paris, Hatier, 1927); *Les Bonnets rouges* (ibid., 1927); *Les Pierres vertes* (Paris, Lemerre, 1931); *La Rose des sables* (Paris, Piazza, 1932).
Le Mercier d'Erm, C. *La Bretagne vue par les écrivains et les artistes* (Paris, Rasmussen, 1929).
Loti, P. *Pêcheur d'Islande* (Paris, Calmann-Levy, 1947); *Mon frère Yves* (ibid., 1947); *Matelot* (ibid., 1947).
Queffelec, H. *Le Recteur de l'île de Sein* (Paris, Stock, 1945); *Au bout du monde* (Paris, Mercure de France, 1949); *Tempête sur Douarnenez* (ibid., 1951); *Un Homme d'Ouessant* (ibid., 1953); *Un feu s'allume sur la mer* (Paris, Amiot-Dumont, 1956); *Un Royaume sous la Mer* (Paris, Presses de la Cite, 1957).
Vissec, L. de *Les Filets Bleus.* n.d.

E. Fisheries, Fishing Craft, and Other Vessels

Almanach du Marin Breton. 1898–1930.
Bellet, A. *La Grande Pêche de la Morue à Terre-Neuve.*
Desmartes, P. *Les Terre-Neuvas.* 1930.
Dupouy, A. *Pêcheurs Bretons.* 1920.

FOLIN. *Bateaux et Navires.* 1892.

JAL. *Archéologie Navale.* 4 vols.

KERZONCUF, J. *La Pêche Maritime.* 1917.

MASSENET, G. *Technique et Pratique des grandes pêches maritimes.*

Mémoires de l'Office Scientifique des Pêches Maritimes:

    (v) RALLIER DU BATY. *La Pêche sur les Bancs de Terre-Neuve et autour des Iles St.-Pierre-Miquelon.*

    (vii) RALLIER DU BATY. *Terre-Neuve et Islande.*

Notes et Rapports de l'Office Scientifique des Recherches des Pêches Maritimes:

    (1) *Rapport sur la Sardine.*

    (26) *Recherches sur la variation de l'iode chez principales laminaires de la côte bretonne.*

    (35) *Les conditions de la Pêche de la Morue sur le Banc de Terre-Neuve.*

    (39) *Etude sur les déplacements de la Pêche du Thon . . .*

    (40) *Compte-rendu . . . dans le Morbihan sur les huitres et leur reproduction.*

    (53) *La Pêche à la Morue.*

PARIS. *Souvenirs de Marine.* 4 vols.

PENFENTENYO, H. de. *L'Industrie Morutière.* 1924.

ROUCH, J. *Pour comprendre la Mer.*

WARINGTON-SMYTH, H. *Mast and Sail in Europe and Asia.* 1929.

PERIODICALS

Annales de Bretagne.

Bulletin de la Société d'histoire et d'archéologie de Bretagne.

Bulletin de la Société Polymathique du Morbihan.

Bulletin de la Société archéologique du Finistère.

Bulletin de la Société d'Emulation des Côtes-du-Nord.

Cahiers de l'Iroise.

INDEX

216 INDEX

MAPS

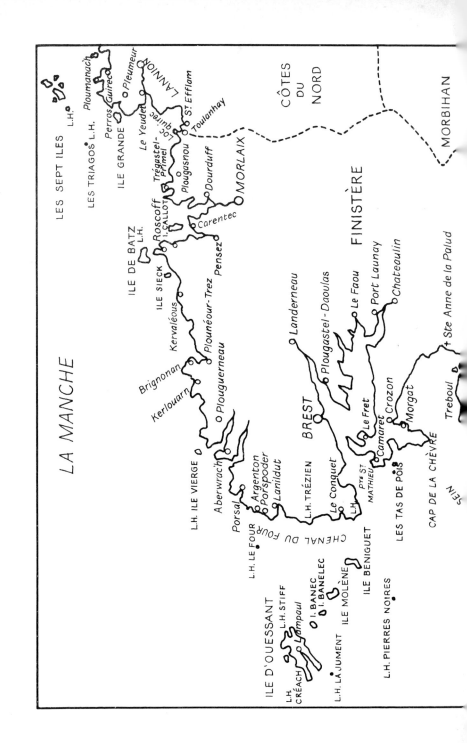

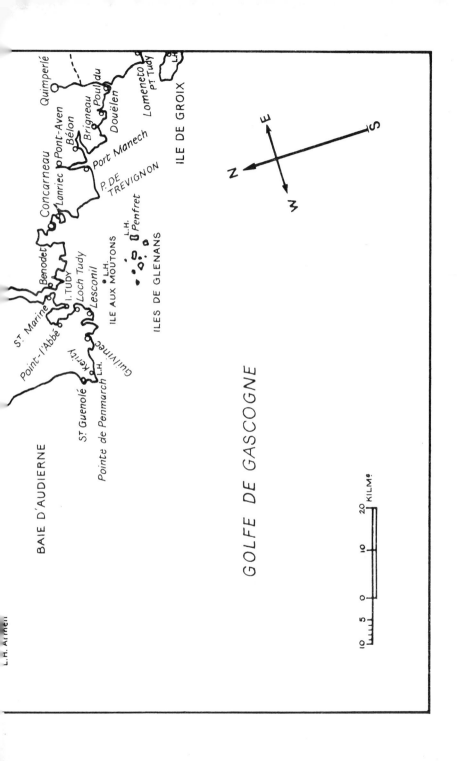

L.H. Armen

BAIE D'AUDIERNE

St. Guenolé
Pointe de Penmarch L.H.

St. Marine
Benodet
Point-l'Abbé
I. TUDY
Loch Tudy
Lesconil
Kerity
Guilvinec

Concarneau
Lanriec
Pont-Aven
Bélon
Brigneau
Poul du
Douëlen
Port Manech
Lomeneto
PT Tudy
Quimperlé

P. DE TREVIGNON

ILE AUX MOUTONS
L.H.
L.H.
Penfret

ILES DE GLENANS

ILE DE GROIX

GOLFE DE GASCOGNE

N   E   W   S

10 5 0 0 10 20 KILM⁹

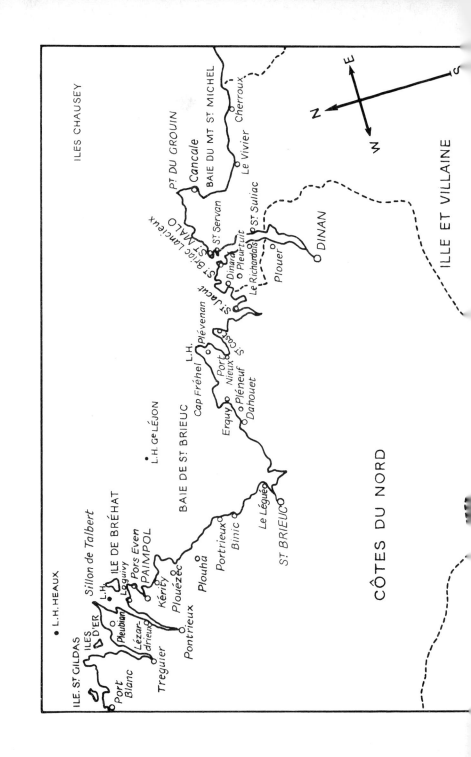

CÔTES DU NORD

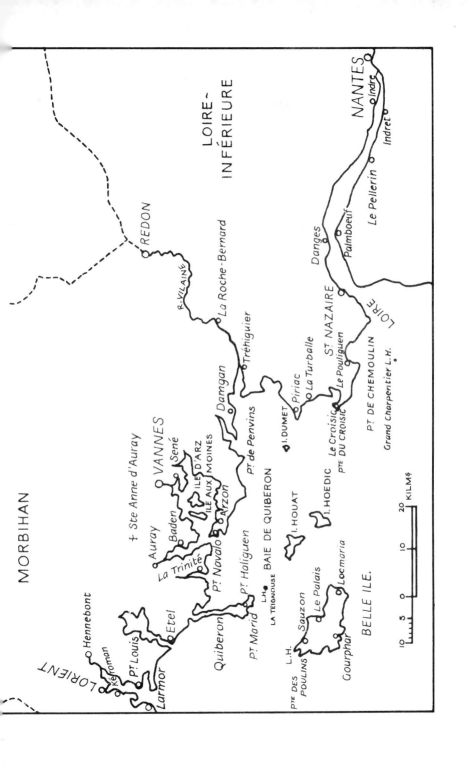